MARY JANE FINSAND

The Complete Diabetic Cookbook

Foreword by James D. Healy, M.D., F.A.A.P.

Sterling Publishing Co., Inc.   New York

"The intention of every other piece of prose may be discussed and even mistrusted; but the purpose of a cookery book is one and unmistakable. Its object can conceivably be no other than to increase the happiness of mankind."

—JOSEPH CONRAD

For Matt J.
who wants to eat "real" food

Library of Congress Cataloging in Publication Data

Finsand, Mary Jane.
The complete diabetic cookbook.

Includes index.
1. Diabetes—Diet therapy—Recipes.   I. Title.
RC662.F56   641.5′6314   79-91382
ISBN 0-8069-5554-6
ISBN 0-8069-5555-4 (lib. bdg.)
ISBN 0-8069-8908-4 (pbk.)

17   19   20   18

Copyright © 1987 by Sterling Publishing Co., Inc.
387 Park Avenue South, New York, N.Y. 10016
Distributed in Canada by Sterling Publishing
% Canadian Manda Group, P.O. Box 920, Station U
Toronto, Ontario, Canada M8Z 5P9
Distributed in Great Britain and Europe by Cassell PLC
Artillery House, Artillery Row, London SW1P 1RT, England
Distributed in Australia by Capricorn Ltd.
P.O. Box 665, Lane Cove, NSW 2066
Manufactured in the United States of America
All rights reserved

Contents

Foreword

The *Complete Diabetic Cookbook* is an invaluable aid in providing a wide range of delicious, nutritious meals for diabetic food management and regulation. Mary Jane has developed a sound, scientific, yet homey, common-sense style of cooking that retains the necessary precise requirements of the diabetic while allowing for considerable individual variety.

The simple food exchange and calorie information will help the diabetic to easily regulate food intake according to a medical doctor's recommendations. In addition, the recipes range from snacks to gourmet dishes; this will allow both youngsters and adults to have variety while still maintaining a proper diet.

Because the United States is in the process of slowly changing to the simple yet scientific metric system, the inclusion of both customary measures (cups, ounces, etc.) and metric measures (millilitres, grams, etc.) expands the versatility of the book. This dual approach will allow the cook to choose the measurement system that is most appropriate. The inclusion of both range/oven cookery and rapid microwave directions is also commendable.

I believe that this book will be useful to diabetics and many other individuals in need of a healthful, common-sense diet. I am grateful to Mary Jane for writing such a comprehensive cookbook.

JAMES D. HEALY, M.D., F.A.A.P.

Introduction

When Matt's diabetes was detected, it seemed only natural (with my background in chemistry, now turned nutritionist) to show I cared—cared enough to respond with a book which would help the beginning as well as the more experienced cooks by adding to their repertoire of diabetic recipes.

No one wants to think of himself as being on a restricted diet, yet all of us are on a diet; therefore, it is the word "restricted" which must be removed. This cookbook is designed to remove the word "restricted," to give a more tasteful and varied food intake for everyone. It is meant to reduce and simplify the day-to-day preparation of healthful good food. There are no complete menus, but rather individual recipes which will open up new cooking horizons. By using the simple exchange or caloric values, anyone can whip up a gourmet meal with no fear of overindulgence.

I am indebted to the countless friends who have given their time, recipes, and their special knowledge in cooking for diabetics. It is because of their help that this cookbook offers exciting adventures in tastes and textures that otherwise would have been lost to the diabetic.

It would be an overstatement to suggest that this cookbook has all the answers to feeding a diabetic. It does not. However, I hope the *Complete Diabetic Cookbook* will help family cooks form everyday good eating habits for the diabetic and for the rest of the family as well.

MARY JANE FINSAND

Using the Recipes for Your Diet

All recipes have been developed using diet substitutions for sugar, syrup, sauces, toppings, puddings, gelatins, mayonnaise, salad dressings, and imitation or lo-cal dairy and non-dairy products.

Remember, diet is the key word for controlling diabetes, and each person's diet is prescribed individually by a doctor or counselor who has been trained to mold your daily life to your diet requirements. DO NOT try to outguess them. If you have any questions about any diabetic recipes, ask your diet counselor.

Read the recipes carefully, then assemble all equipment and ingredients. "Added Touch" ingredients are flavorful additions, but not necessary to the recipe's success. Substitutions or additions of herbs and spices or flavorings to a recipe may be made by using the guide for Spices and Herbs, or for Flavorings and Extracts; they will make any of the recipes distinctively your own.

Use standard measuring equipment (whether metric or customary), be sure to measure accurately. Remember, these recipes are good for everyone, not just the diabetic.

CUSTOMARY TERMS

t.	teaspoon
T.	tablespoon
c.	cup
pkg.	package
pt.	pint
qt.	quart
oz.	ounce
lb.	pound
°F	degrees Fahrenheit
in.	inch

METRIC SYMBOLS

mL	millilitre
L	litre
g	gram
kg	kilogram
mm	millimetre
cm	centimetre
°C	Celsius

GUIDE TO APPROXIMATE EQUIVALENTS

Customary:				Metric:	
ounces; pounds	cups	tablespoons	teaspoons	millilitres	grams; kilograms
			¼ t.	1 mL	
			½ t.	2 mL	
			1 t.	5 mL	
			2 t.	10 mL	
½ oz.		1 T.	3 t.	15 mL	15 g
1 oz.		2 T.	6 t.	30 mL	30 g
2 oz.	¼ c.	4 T.	12 t.	60 mL	
4 oz.	½ c.	8 T.	24 t.	125 mL	
8 oz.	1 c.	16 T.	48 t.	250 mL	
2.2 lb.					1 kg

Keep in mind that this is not an exact conversion, but generally may be used for food measurement.

GUIDE TO PAN SIZES

Baking Pans

Customary:	Metric:	Holds:
8-in. pie	20-cm pie	600 mL
9-in. pie	23-cm pie	1 L
10-in. pie	25-cm pie	1.3 L
8-in. round	20-cm round	1 L
9-in. round	23-cm round	1.5 L
8-in. square	20-cm square	2 L
9-in. square	23-cm square	2.5 L
9 x 5 x 2-in. loaf	23 x 13 x 5-cm loaf	2 L
9-in. tube	23-cm tube	3 L
10-in. tube	25-cm tube	3 L
13 x 9 x 2-in.	33 x 23 x 5-cm	3.5 L
14 x 10-in. cookie tin	35 x 25-cm cookie tin	
15½ x 10½ x 1-in. jelly-roll	39 x 25 x 3-cm jelly-roll	

Cooking Pans and Casseroles

Customary:	Metric:
1 qt.	1 L
2 qt.	2 L
3 qt.	3 L

OVEN COOKING GUIDES

Follow this guide for oven temperature:

Fahrenheit °F	Oven Heat	Celsius °C
250–275°	very slow	120–135°
300–325°	slow	150–165°
350–375°	moderate	177–190°
400–425°	hot	200–220°
450–475°	very hot	230–245°
475–500°	hottest	250–290°

Use this meat thermometer probe guide to check the meat's internal temperature:

Fahrenheit °F	Desired Doneness		Celsius °C
140°	Beef:	rare	60°
150°		medium	65°
170°		well done	75°
160°	Lamb:	medium	70°
170°		well done	75°
180°	Veal:	well done	80°
180°	Pork:	well done	80°
185°	Poultry:	well done	85°

SPICES AND HERBS

Allspice: Cinnamon, ginger, nutmeg flavor; used in breads, pastries, jellies, jams, pickles.

Anise: Licorice flavor; used in candies, breads, fruit, wine, liqueurs.

Basil: Sweet-strong flavor; used in meat, cheese, egg, tomato dishes.

Bay Leaf: Sweet flavor; used in meat, fish, vegetable dishes.

Celery: Unique, pleasantly bitter flavor; used in anything not sweet.

Chive: Light onion flavor; used in anything where onion should be delicate.

Chili Powder: Hot, pungent flavor; used in Mexican, Spanish dishes.

Cinnamon: Pungent, sweet flavor; used in pastries, breads, pickles, wine, beer, liqueurs.

Clove: Pungent, sweet flavor; used for ham, sauces, pastries, puddings, fruit, wine, liqueurs.

Coriander: Butter-lemon flavor; used for pork, cookies, cakes, pies, puddings, fruit, wine and liqueur punches.

Garlic: Strong, aromatic flavor; used in Italian, French, and many meat dishes.

Ginger: Strong, pungent flavor; used in anything sweet, plus with beer, brandy, liqueurs.

Marjoram: Sweet, semi-pungent flavor; used in poultry, lamb, egg, vegetable dishes.

Nutmeg: Sweet, nutty flavor; used in pastries, puddings, vegetables.

Oregano: Sweet, pungent flavor; used in meat, pasta, vegetable dishes.

Paprika: Light, sweet flavor; used in salads, vegetables, poultry, fish, egg dishes; often used to brighten bland-colored casseroles or entrees.

Rosemary: Fresh, sweet flavor; used in soups, meat and vegetable dishes.

Sage: Pungent, bitter flavor; used in stuffings, sausages, some cheese dishes.

Thyme: Pungent, semi-bitter flavor; used in salty dishes or soups.

Woodruff: Sweet vanilla flavor; used in wines, punches.

NOTE: Metric equivalents for the stronger spices and herbs vary for each recipe to allow for individual effectiveness at convenient measurements.

FLAVORINGS AND EXTRACTS

Orange, lime, and lemon peels give vegetables, pastries, and puddings a fresh, clean flavor; liquor flavors, such as brandy or rum, give cakes and other desserts a company flare. Choose from the following to add some zip without calories:

Almond	Butter Rum	Pecan
Anise (Licorice)	Cherry	Peppermint
Apricot	Clove	Pineapple
Banana Crème	Coconut	Raspberry
Blackberry	Grape	Rum
Black Walnut	Hazelnut	Sassafras
Blueberry	Lemon	Sherry
Brandy	Lime	Strawberry
Burnt Sugar	Mint	Vanilla
Butter	Orange	Walnut
Butternut		

APPETIZERS

Fruit Dip

8 oz.	plain lo-cal yogurt	240 g
4 T.	lo-cal preserves	60 mL
½ t.	ground allspice	2 mL
½ t.	lemon juice	2 mL

Combine all ingredients. Whip until fluffy. Chill thoroughly.

Yield: 1 c. (250 mL)
Exchange: 1 milk
Calories: 192

Onion Dip

4 oz.	plain lo-cal yogurt	120 g
¼ c.	onions (finely chopped)	60 mL
1 t.	lemon juice	5 mL
1 T.	parsley	15 mL
dash each	hot pepper sauce, horseradish, salt, pepper	dash each

Combine all ingredients. Chill thoroughly.

Yield: ¾ c. (190 mL)
Exchange: ½ milk
½ vegetable
Calories: 72

Shrimp Dip

5 small	shrimp	5 small
½ t.	Worcestershire sauce	2 mL
1 t.	lemon juice	5 mL
4 oz.	plain lo-cal yogurt	120 g
¼ c.	Chili Sauce (page 129)	60 mL

Crush shrimp. Sprinkle with Worcestershire sauce and lemon juice. Combine yogurt and Chili Sauce. Add crushed shrimp; stir to blend. Chill.

Yield: ¾ c. (190 mL)
Exchange: 1 meat
½ milk
½ fruit
Calories: 108

Avocado Crisps

1	very ripe avocado	1
1 t.	lemon juice	5 mL
1 t.	grated onion	5 mL
1 t.	onion salt	5 mL
1 t.	paprika	5 mL
½ t.	marjoram	2 mL
	thin crackers	

Peel and mash avocado. Add remaining ingredients. Beat until smooth. Spread thinly on crackers.

Yield: 45 servings
Exchange 5 servings: 1 bread
1 fat
Calories 5 servings: 108

Stuffed Celery

2	5-in. (12-cm) stalks celery	2
1 T.	cream cheese (softened)	30 mL
¼ t.	onion powder	1 mL
dash	paprika	dash
	salt and pepper to taste	

Thoroughly rinse and drain celery. Combine cream cheese, onion powder, and paprika. Blend until smooth and creamy. Add salt and pepper. Fill celery stalks. Chill.

Yield: 1 serving
Exchange: 1 fat
Calories: 50

Cheese Appetizers

4 oz.	Cheddar cheese (shredded)	120 g
2 T.	margarine	30 mL
½ c.	flour	125 mL
1 t.	onion (grated)	5 mL
½ t.	salt	2 mL
¼ t.	pepper	1 mL

Blend cheese and margarine until smooth. Add flour, onion, salt, and pepper. Stir until smooth. Shape dough into a roll, 1¼ in. (3.5 cm) in diameter. Wrap in plastic wrap or alumimum foil. Chill. Cut into ¼-in. (6-mm) slices. Bake at 400° F (200° C) for 8 minutes.

Yield: 24 servings
Exchange 1 serving: ½ fat
¼ bread
Calories 1 serving: 37

Cucumbers in Yogurt

1	cucumber	1
1 small	onion	1 small
1 t.	salt	5 mL
½ t.	garlic powder	2 mL
1 t.	lemon juice	5 mL
½ t.	marjoram	2 mL
8 oz.	lo-cal yogurt	240 g

Peel and thinly slice cucumber and onion. Sprinkle with salt. Allow to rest 15 minutes. Drain and pat dry. Combine garlic powder, lemon juice, marjoram, and yogurt; mix thoroughly. Fold in sliced cucumber and onion. Chill.

Yield: 2 c. (500 mL)
Exchange: 1 milk
Calories: 100

Summer Chicken Canapés

4 oz.	ground cooked chicken	120 g
2 T.	margarine (softened)	30 mL
¼ t.	dry mustard	2 mL
½ t.	meat tenderizer	2 mL
½ t.	salt	2 mL
⅛ t.	pepper	1 mL
¼ in. thick	cucumber slices	6 mm thick

Combine chicken, margarine, dry mustard, meat tenderizer, salt, and pepper. Mix thoroughly. Chill. To make canapé: Place 1 t. (5 mL) of chicken mixture in center of cucumber slice.

Yield: 24 servings
Exchange 2 servings: ½ fat
Calories 2 servings: 28

Garlic Bites

1 slice	white bread	1 slice
2 t.	lo-cal margarine	10 mL
¼ t.	garlic powder	2 mL

Remove crust from bread; cut bread into ¼-in. (6-mm) cubes. Melt margarine in small pan. Add garlic powder and heat until sizzling. Add bread cubes; sauté, tossing frequently until brown. Drain and cool.

Yield: 2 servings
Exchange 1 serving: ½ bread
1 fat
Calories 1 serving: 79

Liver Paste

3 oz.	chicken livers	90 g
1 T.	onion (finely chopped)	15 mL
1	egg (hard cooked)	1
2 t.	margarine	10 mL
1 T.	evaporated (regular or skim) milk	15 mL
	salt and pepper to taste	

Boil chicken livers and onion in small amount of water until tender. Drain. Finely chop the egg. Mash livers, onion, egg, and margarine until well blended. Add milk; blend thoroughly. Add salt and pepper.

Yield: 24 servings, 1 t. (5 mL) each
Exchange 3 servings: ½ medium-fat meat
Calories 3 servings: 39

Hors D'Oeuvre Spreads

Yield: ¼ c. (60 mL) spread for 24 crackers or ½ t. (3 mL) per cracker.

Exchange per serving: ½ fat plus cracker exchange

Use one of following as a spread for 24 small crackers:

ANCHOVY

1 oz.	anchovy fillets	30 g
¼ c.	lo-cal margarine	60 mL

Rinse fillets in cold water; pat dry. Grind or chop fine; blend with margarine. Allow to rest.

Exchange ¼ c. (60 mL): 12 fat
1 meat
Calories ¼ c. (60 mL): 250

CAVIAR

2 T.	caviar	30 mL
¼ c.	lo-cal margarine	60 mL

Combine caviar and margarine. Refrigerate overnight.

Exchange ¼ c. (60 mL): 12 fat
1 meat
Calories ¼ c. (60 mL): 280

CRABMEAT

2 T.	crabmeat	30 mL
¼ c.	lo-cal margarine	60 mL

Crush crabmeat; blend with margarine. Refrigerate overnight.

Exchange ¼ c. (60 mL): 12 fat
½ meat
Calories ¼ c. (60 mL): 230

GARLIC

¼ t.	garlic	2 mL
dash	salt	dash
¼ c.	lo-cal margarine	60 mL

Blend ingredients together.

Exchange ¼ c. (60 mL): 12 fat
Calories ¼ c. (60 mL): 200

HERB

dash each	marjoram, oregano, onion (chopped), salt, pepper	dash each
¼ c.	lo-cal margarine	60 mL

Blend ingredients together; allow to **rest** at room temperature 2 hours.

Exchange ¼ c. (60 mL): 12 fat
Calories ¼ c (60 mL): 200

HORSERADISH

1 T.	horseradish (grated)	15 mL
1 t.	parsley (chopped)	5 mL
¼ c.	lo-cal margarine	60 mL

Blend ingredients together; refrigerate overnight.

Exchange ¼ c. (60 mL): 12 fat
Calories ¼ c. (60 mL): 200

LEMON

1 t.	lemon juice	5 mL
dash	salt	dash
¼ t.	parsley	2 mL
¼ c.	lo-cal margarine	60 mL

Blend ingredients together.

Exchange ¼ c. (60 mL): 12 fat
Calories ¼ c. (60 mL): 200

MUSTARD

2 t.	Dijon mustard	10 mL
¼ c.	margarine	60 mL

Blend ingredients together.

Exchange ¼ c. (60 mL): 12 fat
Calories ¼ c. (60 mL): \ 200

NOTE: Exchange and calorie figures above do not include crackers.

Spreads may be topped with 1 t. (5 mL):

Chicken	Salami	Crabmeat
Chicken liver	Sausage	Lobster
Ham	Tuna	

Exchange to add 6 crackers: 1 meat
plus cracker exchange

Bacon   Avocado

Exchange to add 5 crackers: 1 fat
plus cracker exchange

Cauliflower	Mushroom	Green pepper
Celery	Onion	Radish
Cucumber	Parsley	Tomato flesh

Exchange: Only cracker exchange

Smoked Salmon Canapes

8 oz.	smoked salmon	240 g
3 oz.	cream cheese	90 g
½ t.	lemon juice	2 mL
1 t.	milk	5 mL
dash each	thyme, sage, salt, pepper	dash each

Place smoked salmon in blender. Blend until fine. Combine cream cheese, lemon juice, and milk. Stir to make a paste. Add seasonings. Mix well. Add salmon; blend thoroughly. Roll into 22 balls. Chill.

Yield: 22 servings
Exchange 2 servings: 1 meat
Calories 2 servings: 68

Swiss Morsels

8 oz.	Swiss cheese (grated)	240 g
4 oz.	ham (grated)	120 g
2 T.	margarine (softened)	30 mL
¼ t.	thyme	1 mL

Combine all ingredients; mix thoroughly. Shape 2 t. (10 mL) of mixture into a ball. Repeat with remaining mixture.

Yield: 34 servings
Exchange 1 serving: ½ high-fat meat
Calories 1 serving: 51

SOUPS AND STEWS

Chicken Broth

2 lb.	hen (cut up)	1 kg
½ medium	stalk celery (chopped)	½ medium
8 to 10	green onions (chopped)	8 to 10
2 T.	parsley (chopped)	30 mL
2 t.	salt	10 mL
1 t.	thyme	5 mL
1 t.	marjoram	5 mL
½ t.	pepper	2 mL

Wash chicken pieces; place in large kettle. Cover with 2 qt. (2 L) water; bring to boil, cover and cook 1 hour or until chicken is tender. Add remaining ingredients; simmer 1 hour. Remove chicken; strain broth. Refrigerate broth overnight. Remove all fat from surface before reheating broth.

Yield: 2 qt. (2 L) broth
Exchange: Negligible
Calories: Negligible

Beef Broth

3 to 4 lb.	beef soup bones or chuck roast	1½ to 2 kg
½ stalk	celery (chopped)	½ stalk
3	carrots (sliced)	3
1 medium	onion (chopped)	1 medium
½	green pepper (chopped)	½
2	bay leaves	2
½ t. each	thyme, marjoram, paprika, pepper	2 mL each
2 t.	salt	10 mL

Place beef in large kettle; cover with 2 qt. (2 L) water. Bring to a boil, cover and cook 2 hours, or until meat is tender. Add remaining ingredients; simmer 1 hour. Remove beef; strain broth. Refrigerate broth overnight. Remove all fat from surface before reheating broth.

Yield: 2 qt. (2 L) broth
Exchange: Negligible
Calories: Negligible

Broth with Vegetables

Cook ½ c. (125 mL) vegetables or combination of vegetables in boiling salted water; drain. Add to hot broth just before serving.

Microwave: Add ½ c. (125 mL) vegetables (no water needed). Cook on High for 3 minutes. Add to hot broth just before serving.

Yield: ½ c. (125 mL)
Exchange: ½ vegetable
Calories: 18

Broth with Noodles

Cook ¼ c. (60 mL) noodles or broken spaghetti in boiling salted water; drain. Add to hot broth just before serving.

Microwave: Add ¼ c (60 mL) noodles or pasta to 2 c. (500 mL) boiling salted water. Cook on High for 3 minutes. Hold 3 minutes. Drain. Add to hot broth just before serving.

Yield: ½ c. (125 mL)
Exchange: 1 bread
Calories: 68

Broth Orientale

2 T.	rice	30 mL
1½ c.	vegetable broth	375 mL
1 T.	celery (thinly sliced)	15 mL
½ t.	onion (finely chopped)	3 mL
1 T.	bean sprouts	15 mL
1	water chestnut (thinly sliced)	1
	salt to taste	

Add rice to cold vegetable broth; bring to boil. Reduce heat; simmer 20 minutes. Add celery, onion, bean sprouts and water chestnut; simmer 10 minutes. Add salt.

Microwave: Add rice to cold broth; heat to a boil. Cover. Hold 15 minutes. Add remaining ingredients, except salt. Cook 3 minutes. Hold 5 minutes. Add salt.

Yield: 1¼ c (310 mL)
Exchange: ⅛ bread
⅛ vegetable
Calories: 11

Broth Italiano

⅛ c.	vermicelli (broken)	30 mL
1 c.	broth	250 mL
1 oz.	thinly sliced prosciutto (shredded)	30 g
⅛ t.	garlic powder	1 mL
⅛ t.	marjoram	1 mL
1 T.	Parmesan cheese (grated)	15 mL

Cook vermicelli in boiling salted water; drain and rinse. Bring broth to boil. Add prosciutto, garlic powder, and marjoram. Simmer 5 minutes. Add vermicelli. Pour into bowl. Sprinkle Parmesan cheese over top.

Yield: 1¼ c. (310 mL)
Exchange: ½ bread
1 medium-fat meat
Calories: 107

Broth Madeira

Add 1 T. (15 mL) Madeira to 1 c. (250 mL) broth. Bring just to a boil. Garnish with lemon slice and fresh chopped parsley.

Microwave: Add 1 T. (15 mL) Madeira to 1 c. (250 mL) broth. Cook on High for 2 minutes. Garnish with lemon slice and fresh chopped parsley.

Yield: 1 c. (250 mL)
Exchange: Negligible
Calories: Negligible

Vegetable Broth

1 c.	onion (chopped)	250 mL
2 c.	carrots (diced)	500 mL
1 c.	celery (chopped)	250 mL
2 c.	spinach (cut in small pieces)	500 mL
2 c.	tomato (peeled and chopped)	500 mL
1	bay leaf	1
2 T.	parsley or parsley flakes	30 mL
½ t.	thyme	3 mL
1 blade	mace	1 blade
¼ t.	garlic or garlic powder	1 mL
1 T.	Worcestershire	15 mL
	salt to taste	

Place vegetables in large kettle. Cover with 2 to 3 qt. (2 to 3 L) water. Bring to boil; reduce heat and simmer for 2 hours. Stir frequently. Add seasonings. Simmer 1 hour. Strain. Add water to make 2 qt. (2 L).

Yield: 2 qt. (2 L) broth
Exchange: Negligible
Calories: Negligible

Tomato Beef Bouillon

2 T.	margarine	30 mL
¼ c.	onion (chopped)	60 mL
46 oz.	tomato juice	1½ L
2 cans	beef broth **or**	2 cans
2½ c.	homemade beef broth	625 mL
1	bay leaf	1
1 t.	salt	5 mL
½ t.	pepper	2 mL

Heat margarine in large saucepan. Add onion and cook until tender. Add tomato juice, beef broth (canned or home-made), bay leaf, salt, and pepper; heat thoroughly.
DO NOT BOIL. Remove bay leaf. Ladle into warm bowls.

Added Touch: Top each serving with 1 t. (5 mL) grated American cheese.

Yield: 8 servings, 1 c. (250 mL) each
Exchange 1 serving: ¼ vegetable
1 fat
Calories 1 serving: 58

Greek Egg Lemon Soup

2 qt.	chicken broth	2 L
3	eggs (separated)	3
	juice of 1 lemon	

Bring broth to a boil in saucepan. Beat egg whites until stiff. Add egg yolks. Beat slowly until mixture is a light yellow. Add lemon juice gradually, beating constantly. Pour small amount of chicken broth into egg mixture. Pour egg mixture into hot broth, beating constantly.

Yield: 8 servings, 1 c. (250 mL) each
Exchange 1 serving: ¼ high-fat meat
Calories 1 serving: 27

Quick Egg Soup

1½ c.	boiling water	375 mL
1 cube	vegetable bouillon	1 cube
1	egg	1

Dissolve bouillon cube in boiling water; remove from heat. Beat egg; blend into vegetable broth. Reheat slowly. DO NOT BOIL.

Yield: 1½ c. (375 mL)
Exchange: 1 medium-fat meat
Calories: 80

German Cabbage Soup

2 oz.	ground beef round	60 g
2 T.	onion (grated)	30 mL
dash each	mustard, soy sauce, salt, pepper	dash each
1 T.	dry red wine	15 mL
1¼ c.	beef broth	300 mL
2 large	cabbage leaves (cut in pieces)	2 large
½ medium	tomato (cubed)	½ medium
½ t.	fresh parsley (chopped)	2 mL

Combine ground round, onion, mustard, soy sauce, salt, and pepper; mix thoroughly. Form into tiny meatballs. Add wine to broth; bring to boil. Add meatballs to broth, one at a time. Bring to boil again. Cook meatballs 5 minutes; remove to soup bowl. Add cabbage and tomatoes to broth. Simmer 5 minutes. Pour over meatballs. Garnish with parsley.

Yield: 1½ c. (375 mL)
Exchange: 1 medium-fat meat
          ½ vegetable
Calories: 55

Borsch

16-oz. can	beets with juice	500-g can
2 T.	sugar replacement	30 mL
¾ t.	salt	3 mL
3 T.	lemon juice	45 mL
½ t.	thyme	2 mL
1	egg (well beaten)	1

Puree beets in blender. Add enough water to make 1 qt. (1 L). Pour into saucepan. Add sugar replacement, salt, lemon juice, and thyme; heat to a boil. Remove from heat. Add small amount of hot beet mixture to egg. Stir egg mixture into beet mixture. Return to heat; cook and stir until hot.

Yield: 4 servings, 1 c. (250 mL) each
Exchange 1 serving: 1 bread
ONE ¼ high-fat meat
Calories 1 serving: 104
Added touch: Top each serving with 1 t. (5 mL) local sour cream.

French Meatball Soup

2 T.	rice (uncooked)	30 mL
2 oz.	ground beef round	60 g
1 T.	egg (raw, beaten)	15 mL
1 t.	onion (grated)	5 mL
dash each	garlic, parsley, nutmeg	dash each
2 T.	dry red wine	30 mL
1¼ c.	beef broth	300 mL
	salt and pepper to taste	

Add rice to 1 c. (250 mL) salted water. Boil 5 minutes; drain well. Blend rice, ground round, egg, onion, garlic, parsley, and nutmeg; form into small meatballs. Add wine to broth; bring to a boil. Drop meatballs into hot broth, one at a time. Bring to boil again; reduce heat. Simmer 20 minutes. Add salt and pepper.

Microwave: Add rice to 1 c. (250 mL) salted water. Bring to a boil. Hold 5 minutes; drain well. Combine meatball ingredients as above. Bring wine and broth to a boil. Drop meatballs into hot broth, one at a time. Bring to a boil again. Hold 10 minutes. Add salt and pepper.

Yield: 1½ c. (375 mL)
Exchange: 1 medium-fat meat
½ bread
Calories: 71

Ham and Split Pea Soup

2 lb.	meaty ham bone	1 kg
1	bay leaf	1
2 c.	dried green split peas	500 mL
1 c.	onions (chopped)	250 mL
1 c.	celery (cubed)	250 mL
1 c.	carrots (grated)	250 mL
	salt and pepper to taste	

Cover ham bone and bay leaf with water. Simmer for 2 to 2½ hours. Remove bone and strain liquid. Refrigerate overnight. Remove lean meat from bone; set aside. Remove fat from surface of liquid. Heat liquid; add enough water to make 2½ qt. (2½ L). Add peas; simmer for 20 minutes. Remove from heat and allow to stand 1 hour. Add onions, celery, carrots, and lean pieces of ham. Add salt and pepper. Simmer for 40 minutes. Stir occasionally.

Yield: 10 servings
Exchange 1 serving: ½ high-fat meat
1 vegetable
Calories 1 serving: 204

Cream of Chicken and Almond Soup

1 c.	chicken broth	250 mL
1	whole clove	1
1 sprig	parsley	1 sprig
½	bay leaf	½
pinch	mace	pinch
1 T.	celery (sliced)	15 mL
1 T.	carrot (diced)	15 mL
1 t.	onion (diced)	5 mL
2 t.	stale bread crumbs	10 mL
½ oz.	chicken breast (cubed)	15 g
1 t.	blanched almonds (crushed)	5 mL
¼ c.	skim milk	60 mL
1 t.	flour	5 mL
	salt and pepper to taste	

Heat chicken broth, clove, parsley, bay leaf, and mace to a boil; remove from heat. Allow to rest 10 minutes; strain. Add celery, carrot, onion, bread crumbs, chicken, and almonds to seasoned chicken broth; simmer 20 minutes. Blend in skim milk and flour. Remove soup from heat; add milk mixture. Return to heat. Simmer (do not boil) 3 to 5 minutes. Add salt and pepper.

Yield: 1½ c. (375 mL)
Exchange: ½ lean meat
1 vegetable
¼ milk
Calories: 89

Crab Chowder

1 c.	milk	250 mL
1 t.	flour	5 mL
¼ c.	water	60 mL
¼ c.	cooked crabmeat (flaked)	60 mL
3 T.	mushroom pieces	45 mL
3 T.	asparagus pieces	**45 mL**
	salt and pepper to taste	

Blend milk, flour, and water thoroughly; pour into saucepan. Add crabmeat, mushrooms, and asparagus. Cook over low heat until slightly thickened. Add salt and pepper.

Yield: 1 c. (250 mL)
Exchange: 1 milk
1 vegetable
1 lean meat
Calories: 150

Clam Chowder

1 slice	bacon	1 slice
1½ c.	fish or vegetable broth	375 mL
2 T.	carrot (diced)	30 mL
1 T.	onion (diced)	15 mL
1 T.	celery (diced)	15 mL
1 large	tomato (diced)	1 large
1 medium	potato (diced)	1 medium
dash each	thyme, rosemary, salt, pepper	dash each
1 t.	flour	5 mL
¼ c.	water	60 mL
1 oz.	clams	30 g

Cook bacon until crisp; drain and crumble. Combine broth, carrot, onion, celery, tomato, potato, and seasonings. Simmer until vegetables are tender. Blend flour and water; stir into chowder. Reduce heat. Add clams and crumbled bacon. Heat to thicken slightly.

Microwave: Combine vegetables with broth and seasonings; cover. Cook on High for 4 minutes, or until vegetables are tender. Add flour-water mixture. Cook 30 seconds; stir. Add clams and bacon; stir. Cook 30 seconds. Hold 3 minutes.

Yield: 2 c. (500 mL)
Exchange: 1 lean meat
1 fat
1 vegetable
1 bread
Calories: 200

Fish Chowder

2 c.	water	500 mL
3 oz.	bullhead fillet	90 g
1 medium	potato (diced)	1 medium
3 T.	onion (diced)	45 mL
3 T.	celery (diced)	45 mL
2 T.	carrot (diced)	30 mL
1 medium	tomato (diced)	1 medium
	salt and pepper to taste	

Combine all ingredients in saucepan. Heat to a boil; cover and reduce heat. Simmer 1 to 1½ hours.

Yield: 3 servings, 1 c. (250 mL) each
Exchange 1 serving: 1 medium-fat meat
½ vegetable
½ bread
Calories 1 serving: 81

Oyster Stew

1 t.	flour	5 mL
1 T.	celery (minced)	15 mL
1 t.	salt	5 mL
dash each	Worcestershire sauce, soy sauce	dash each
1 T.	water	15 mL
1 oz.	oysters (with liquid)	30 g
1 t.	butter	5 mL
1 c.	skim milk	250 mL

Blend flour, celery, seasonings, and water in saucepan; add oysters with liquid, and butter. Simmer over low heat until edges of oysters curl. Remove from heat; add skim milk. Reheat over low heat. Add extra salt if desired.

Yield: 1½ c. (375 mL)
Exchange: 1 lean meat
1 milk
¼ bread
Calories: 220

Kidney Stew

2 oz.	beef kidney (cooked)	60 g
1½ c.	beef broth	375 mL
3 T.	leek (chopped)	45 mL
1 slice	bacon (cooked and drained)	1 slice
¼ c.	mushrooms	60 mL
3 T.	green pepper (sliced)	45 mL
dash each	parsley, thyme, tarragon, salt, pepper	dash each

Heat all ingredients to a boil. Reduce heat and simmer until green pepper slices are tender.

Yield: 1½ c. (375 mL)
Exchange: 2 lean meat
1 fat
Calories: 130

Pizza Stew

1 oz.	Canadian bacon	30 g
1½ c.	Tomato Sauce (p. 128)	375 mL
¼ c.	water	60 mL
2 T.	onion (chopped)	30 mL
1 T.	mushroom pieces	15 mL
1 T.	black olives (pitted and chopped)	15 mL
1 T.	celery (chopped)	15 mL.
1 T.	green pepper (chopped)	15 mL
dash each	oregano, garlic powder, salt to taste	dash each
½ c.	elbow macaroni (cooked)	125 mL

Fry Canadian bacon; drain and cut away any fat. Heat Tomato Sauce and water to a boil. Add bacon, vegetables, and seasonings. Cook until vegetables are tender. Add macaroni; reheat.

Yield: 2¼ c. (560 mL)
Exchange: 1 high-fat meat
1 bread
1 vegetable
Calories: 275

Bean Stew

1 T.	pinto beans	15 mL
1 T.	northern beans	15 mL
1 T.	lentils	15 mL
1 c.	beef broth	250 mL
1 T.	carrot (sliced)	15 mL
1 T.	hominy	15 mL
1 t.	onion (diced)	5 mL
½ t.	green chilies (chopped)	2 mL
dash each	garlic powder, oregano, salt, pepper	dash each

Boil beans and lentils in beef broth for 10 minutes, covered. Allow to stand 1 to 2 hours, or overnight. Place softened beans and remaining ingredients in baking dish. Bake at 350° F (175° C) for 45 minutes to 1 hour, or until ingredients are tender.

Microwave: Place beans and lentils in beef broth; cover. Cook on High for 5 minutes. Allow to stand 1 to 2 hours or overnight. Add remaining ingredients. Cook on Medium for 10 to 15 minutes, or until ingredients are tender.

Yield: 1½ c. (375 mL)
Exchange: 1 lean meat
2 bread
Calories: 225

Zucchini Meatball Stew

1 oz.	ground beef	30 g
½ c.	ground zucchini	125 mL
1 t.	onion (finely chopped)	5 mL
1	egg	1
¼ c.	rice (uncooked)	60 mL
dash each	oregano, cumin, garlic salt, pepper	dash each
1 c.	beef broth	250 mL
1 large	tomato (diced)	1 large
1 t.	parsley (chopped)	5 mL
	salt and pepper to taste	

Combine ground beef, zucchini, onion, egg, rice, and seasonings; mix thoroughly. Shape into small meatballs. Combine beef broth, tomato, and parsley in saucepan; heat to boil. Drop meatballs into hot broth, one at a time. Cover and simmer 30 to 40 minutes. Add salt and pepper.

Microwave: Cook beef broth, tomato, and parsley on High for 3 minutes, covered. Drop meatballs into broth. Cook on High 5 minutes. Hold 10 minutes. Add salt and pepper.

Yield: 1¾ c. (430 mL)
Exchange: 2 medium-fat meat
1 vegetable
1 bread
Calories: 203

Chicken Giblet Stew

3 oz.	chicken giblets	90 g
2 c.	water	500 mL
¼ t.	thyme	2 mL
¼	bay leaf	¼
⅛ t.	parsley (crushed)	1 mL
	salt and pepper to taste	
3 T.	potatoes (diced)	45 mL
2 T.	onions (diced)	30 mL
2 T.	celery (diced)	30 mL
2 T.	green beans (sliced)	30 mL
2 T.	carrots (diced)	30 mL
2 T.	peas	30 mL
1 t.	flour	5 mL
¼ c.	water	60 mL

Remove center muscle of giblets. Place the 2 c. water, giblets, and seasonings in saucepan; cover. Heat to a boil; reduce heat and simmer until giblets are tender, about 1 hour. Add extra water to make about 2 c. (500 mL) liquid. Remove bay leaf. Add vegetables; reheat and cook until vegetables

are tender. Blend flour with the ¼ c. water. Blend into stew.
Cook to desired thickness.

Yield: 3 servings, 1 cup (250 mL) each
Exchange 1 serving: 1 lean meat
                        1 bread
                        1 vegetable
Calories 1 serving: 120

Pepper Pot
(Leftovers may be used)

2 oz.	lean pork, cut in 1-in. (2.5-cm) cubes	60 g
1 oz.	beef, cut in 1-in. (2.5-cm) cubes	30 g
1 oz.	chicken, cut in 1-in. (2.5-cm) cubes	30 g
¼ c.	carrot pieces	60 mL
¼ c.	onion slices	60 mL
¼ c.	celery pieces	60 mL
¼ c.	potatoes (cubed)	60 mL
½ c.	water	125 mL
1 t.	flour	5 mL
dash each	curry powder, garlic powder, salt, pepper	dash each

Brown pork and beef cubes slowly in frying pan. Add
chicken cubes for last few minutes; drain. Place meat, carrots, onions, celery, and potatoes in individual baking dish.
Combine water, flour, and seasonings in screwtop jar; shake
to blend well. Pour over meat mixture. Cover tightly and
bake at 350° F (175° C) for 45 minutes to 1 hour, or until
meat is tender and gravy has thickened.

Microwave: Reduce water to ¼ c. (60 mL). Cover. Cook on
High for 10 minutes. Hold 5 minutes.

Yield: 1 serving
Exchange: 4 high-fat meat
               1 vegetable
               1 bread
Calories: 418

Stefado

1 stick	cinnamon	1 stick
1	bay leaf	1
5	whole cloves	5
12 oz.	beef roast (cubed)	360 g
	salt and pepper to taste	
1 t.	margarine	5 mL
1½ c.	onions (sliced)	375 mL
3 medium	tomatoes (peeled and cubed)	3 medium
½ c.	red wine	125 mL
1 t.	brown sugar replacement	5 mL
2 T.	raisins	30 mL
1 c.	water	250 mL
1	garlic clove (crushed)	1

Place cinnamon, bay leaf, and cloves in small cheesecloth bag. Combine with remaining ingredients in soup kettle; cook 1 to 1½ hours until meat is tender. Remove spice bag before serving.

Microwave: Same as above. Cook on High 15 to 20 minutes.

Yield: 3 servings, 1 c. (250 mL)) each
Exchange 1 serving: 4 high-fat meat
1 vegetable
Calories 1 serving: 430

CASSEROLES
AND
ONE-DISH MEALS

Beef Stroganoff

3 oz.	lean beef (cubed)	90 g
1 t.	margarine	5 mL
½	onion (cut into large pieces)	½
¼ t.	garlic (minced)	1 mL
2 T.	mushroom pieces	30 mL
½ c.	condensed cream of mushroom soup	125 mL
1 T.	lo-cal sour cream	15 mL
1 t.	ketchup	5 mL
dash each	Worcestershire sauce, ground bay leaf, salt, pepper	dash each
1 c.	noodles	250 mL

Brown beef cubes in margarine. Add onion, garlic, and mushrooms. Cook over low heat until onion is partially cooked; remove from heat. Combine condensed soup, sour cream, ketchup, and seasonings; blend well. Pour over beef mixture; heat thoroughly. (DO NOT BOIL.) Serve over noodles.

Yield: 1 serving
Exchange: 3 high-fat meat
2½ bread
Calories: 470

Packaged Steak Supper

3 oz.	beef minute steak	90 g
1 small	potato	1 small
2 T.	carrot (sliced)	30 mL
2 T.	onion (sliced)	30 mL
2 T.	celery (sliced)	30 mL
2 large	tomato slices	2 large
	salt and pepper to taste	

Place steak on large piece of aluminum foil. Layer vegetables in order given. Add salt and pepper. Wrap in foil, sealing ends securely. Bake at 350° F (175° C) for 1 hour.

Microwave: Place in plastic wrap. Cook on High for 10 minutes.

Yield: 1 serving
Exchange: 3 medium-fat meat
1 bread
½ vegetable
Calories: 375

Quick Kabobs

2 oz.	cooked beef roast, cut in 1-in. (2.5-cm) cubes	60 g
6	green peppers, cut in 1-in. (2.5-cm) squares	6
6	cherry tomatoes	6
6	zucchini, cut in 1-in. (2.5-cm) cubes	30 mL
6	unsweetened pineapple chunks	6
2 T.	lo-cal French dressing	6

Alternate beef, vegetables, and fruit on 2 skewers. Brush with 1 T. (15 mL) of the French dressing. Broil 5 to 6 in. (12 to 15 cm) from heat for 8 minutes. Brush with remaining French dressing. Broil 4 minutes longer.

Yield: 1 serving (2 kabobs)
Exchange: 2 medium-fat meat
1 vegetable
1 fruit
Calories: 150

Beef and Rice Casserole

3 oz.	ground beef	90 g
1 T.	onion (chopped)	15 mL
1 T.	celery (chopped)	15 mL
¾ c.	condensed chicken gumbo soup	180 mL
¼ c.	water	60 mL
½ c.	rice (uncooked)	125 mL
¼ c.	condensed cream of mushroom soup	60 mL
	salt and pepper to taste	

Combine ground beef, onion, and celery with a small amount of water in a saucepan. Boil until onion is tender; drain. Combine condensed chicken gumbo soup, water, and rice. Simmer until all moisture is absorbed. Mix beef mixture, rice, and mushroom soup; pour into a small greased casserole dish. Add salt and pepper. Bake at 350° F (175° C) for 25 minutes.

Microwave: Cook on Medium for 8 to 10 minutes.

Yield: 1 serving
Exchange: 3 high-fat meat
2 bread
Calories: 380

German Goulash

3 oz.	lean ground beef	90 g
1 t.	onion (chopped)	5 mL
1 T.	green pepper (chopped)	15 mL
1 T.	celery (chopped)	15 mL
¼	bay leaf (crushed)	¼
½ c.	kidney beans (cooked)	125 mL
½ c.	elbow macaroni (cooked)	125 mL
¼ c.	carrot (sliced)	60 mL
	salt and pepper to taste	

Brown ground beef, onion, green pepper, and celery over low heat; drain. Add crushed bay leaf, kidney beans, macaroni, and carrots; mix gently. Add salt and pepper. Pour into casserole dish; cover. Bake at 350° F (175° C) for 40 minutes.

Microwave: Cook on Medium for 7 minutes.

Yield: 1 serving
Exchange: 3 medium-fat meat
                 2½ bread
Calories: 413

Stuffed Peppers

1	green pepper	1
2 T.	rice	30 mL
2 oz.	lean ground beef	60 g
1	egg	1
1 t.	onion flakes	5 mL
1 T.	mushrooms (finely chopped)	15 mL
	salt and pepper to taste	
1 t.	Tomato Sauce (p. 128)	5 mL

Cut green pepper in half, lengthwise. Remove membrane and seeds; rinse, drain and reserve shells. Boil rice with ½ c. (125 mL) of water for 5 minutes; drain. Combine ground beef, rice, egg, onion flakes, and mushrooms; blend thoroughly. Add salt and pepper. Fill green pepper cavities with beef mixture; top with Tomato Sauce. Place in baking dish; cover. Bake at 350° F (175° C) for 20 to 25 minutes.

Microwave: Cook on High for 10 minutes.

Yield: 1 serving
Exchange: 3 medium-fat meat
                 1 bread
                 1 vegetable
Calories: 255

Lasagne

2 oz.	ground beef	60 g
1 T.	onion (chopped)	15 mL
½ c.	Tomato Sauce (p. 128)	125 mL
3 T.	water	45 mL
¼ t.	garlic powder	1 mL
½ t.	oregano	3 mL
	salt and pepper to taste	
1½ c.	lasagne noodles (cooked)	375 mL
1 oz.	mozzarella cheese (grated)	30 g
1 oz.	provolone cheese (grated)	30 g

Crumble beef in small amount of water; add onion. Boil until meat is cooked; drain. Blend Tomato Sauce, 3 T. (45 mL) water, garlic powder, oregano, salt, and pepper. Add beef-onion mixture; stir to blend. Spread small amount of sauce into bottom of individual baking dish. Layer noodles, sauce, mozzarella and provolone cheese. Bake at 375° F (190° C) for 30 minutes.

Microwave: Cook on High for 10 minutes.

Yield: 1 serving
Exchange: 4 high-fat meat
3 bread
Calories: 485

Hamburger Pie

2 lb.	lean ground beef	1 kg
½ c.	cornflakes (crushed)	125 mL
¼ t.	garlic powder	1 mL
½ t.	onion (finely chopped)	3 mL
1	egg	1
	salt and pepper to taste	
2¼ c.	water	560 mL
1 c.	skim milk	250 mL
1 t.	salt	5 mL
2 c.	instant mashed potatoes	500 mL
1 t.	margarine	5 mL

Combine ground beef, cornflakes, garlic powder, onion, and egg; mix well. Add salt and pepper. Place beef mixture in 9-in. (23-cm) pie pan. Pat to cover bottom and sides evenly. Bake at 425° F (220° C) for 30 minutes; drain off excess fat. Heat water, skim milk, and salt just to a boil; remove from heat. Add potato granules; mix thoroughly. Add margarine; blend well. Cover and allow to stand 5 minutes, or until potatoes thicken. Spread evenly over meat mixture. Return to oven and bake until potatoes are golden brown. Allow to rest 10 minutes before cutting pie into wedges.

Microwave: Cover beef mixture. Cook on Medium for 10 to 12 minutes; drain. Cover with potatoes. Cook on Medium for 2 minutes. Hold 5 minutes.

Yield: 8 servings
Exchange 1 serving: 4 high-fat meat
1 bread
½ fat
Calories 1 serving: 372

Wiener-Egg Scramble

1 slice	bacon	1 slice
1 t.	onion (chopped)	5 mL
1	wiener (sliced)	1
½ t.	green pepper (chopped)	2 mL
1	egg	1
1 t.	skim milk	5 mL
dash	Worcestershire sauce	dash

Cook bacon until crisp; drain bacon and pan. Crumble bacon. Place bacon, onion, wiener, and green pepper in pan. Sauté on low heat until onion is tender. Beat egg with skim milk and Worcestershire sauce; pour over wiener mixture. Cook until set.

Yield: 1 serving
Exchange: 2 high-fat meat
2 fat
Calories: 170

Cheese Lasagne

½ c.	Tomato Sauce (p. 128)	125 mL
3 T.	water	45 mL
1 T.	onion	15 mL
¼ t.	garlic powder	1 mL
½ t.	oregano	3 mL
	salt and pepper to taste	
¼ c.	large curd cottage cheese	60 mL
1	egg	1
1½ c.	lasagne noodles (cooked)	375 mL
2 oz.	mozzarella cheese	60 g
1 T.	Parmesan cheese	15 mL

Combine Tomato Sauce, water, onion, garlic powder, oregano, salt, and pepper. Thoroughly blend together cottage cheese and egg. Spread small amount of sauce into bottom of individual baking dish. Alternate layers of noodles, sauce, cottage cheese mixture, and mozzarella cheese. Top with Parmesan cheese. Bake at 375° F (190° C) for 30 mnutes.

Microwave: Cook on High for 10 minutes.

Yield: 1 serving
Exchange: 3 high-fat meat
3 bread
Calories: 350

Clam Pilaf

2 oz.	clams (minced)	60 g
½ c.	rice (cooked)	125 mL
2 T.	onion (chopped)	30 mL
1 medium	fresh tomato (peeled and cubed)	1 medium
dash each	ground bay leaf, thyme, salt, pepper	dash each
2 T.	grated Cheddar cheese	30 mL

Combine clams, rice, onion, tomato, and seasonings in baking dish; top with cheese. Bake at 350° F (175° C) for 25 minutes.

Microwave: Combine clams, rice, onion, tomato, and seasonings. Cook on High for 5 minutes; top with cheese. Reheat on High for 1 minute.

Yield: 1 serving
Exchange: 2 lean meat
1 bread
Calories: 170

Macaroni and Cheese Supreme

1 c.	elbow macaroni	250 mL
11-oz. can	condensed cream of mushroom soup	300-g can
6 oz.	cheese (shredded)	180 mL
1 t.	yellow mustard	5 mL
1 t.	salt	5 mL
dash	pepper	dash
2 c.	cooked spinach (drained)	500 mL
12 oz.	lean meat (diced)	360 g

Cook macaroni as directed on package; drain. Combine mushroom soup, cheese, mustard, salt, and pepper. Add macaroni; stir well. Spread cooked spinach on bottom of lightly greased 13 x 9-in. (33 x 23-cm) baking dish. Top with meat. Spoon macaroni mixture evenly over entire surface. Bake at 375° F (190° C) for 40 minutes. Allow to cool 15 minutes before serving.

Microwave: Cook on Medium for 12 to 15 minutes. Turn dish halfway through cooking time. Allow to rest 15 minutes before serving.

Yield: 6 servings
Exchange 1 serving: 2 bread
3 high-fat meat
1 vegetable
Calories 1 serving: 287

Turkey à la King

1 T.	green pepper (diced)	15 mL
2 T.	celery (sliced)	30 mL
¼ c.	condensed cream of chicken soup	60 mL
2 T.	skim milk	30 mL
2 T.	mushrooms (chopped)	30 mL
3 oz.	cooked turkey (diced)	90 g
1 T.	pimiento (chopped)	15 mL
	salt and pepper to taste	
2 slices	bread (toasted)	2 slices

Cook green pepper and celery in boiling water until tender; drain. Blend condensed soup and skim milk. Add green pepper, celery, mushrooms, turkey, and pimiento. Add salt and pepper. Heat slightly over low heat. Cut toast into triangles; place in small bowl, tips up. Spoon turkey mixture over tips.

Yield: 1 serving
Exchange: 3 medium-fat meat
2¼ bread
¼ vegetable
Calories: 450

Turkey à la King II

¼ c.	White Sauce (p. 134)	60 mL
1 oz.	cooked turkey (diced)	30 g
¼ c.	mushroom pieces	60 mL
2 T.	green pepper (chopped)	30 mL
1 T.	stuffed green olives (chopped)	15 mL
	salt and pepper to taste	
	dough for 1 baking powder biscuit (p. 88)	

Heat White Sauce. Combine sauce, turkey, mushrooms, green pepper, and olives; add salt and pepper. Pour into lightly greased individual baking dish. Top with biscuit dough. Bake at 375° F (190° C) for 15 to 20 minutes, or until biscuit is golden brown.

Yield: 1 serving
Exchange: 1 medium-fat meat
              1 vegetable
              1 bread
Calories: 168

Chicken Gambeano

¼ c.	condensed cream of chicken soup	60 mL
3 T.	skim milk	45 mL
¼ c.	zucchini (cubed)	60 mL
¼ c.	green beans	60 mL
2 oz.	cooked chicken (cubed)	60 g
¼ t.	poultry seasoning	2 mL
	salt and pepper to taste	
1¼ c.	linguine (cooked)	310 mL

Blend condensed soup and skim milk; place in saucepan. Add zucchini and green beans. Cook over Medium heat until vegetables are partially tender. Add chicken and seasonings; reheat. Serve over linguine.

Microwave: Blend condensed soup and skim milk in bowl. Add zucchini and green beans; cover. Cook on High for 5 to 7 minutes, or until vegetables are partially tender. Add chicken and seasonings; reheat on Medium for 4 minutes. Serve over linguine.

Yield: 1 serving
Exchange: 3 bread
              2 medium-fat meat
              ½ vegetable
Calories: 300

Mostaccioli with Oysters

8-oz. can	oysters with liquid (minced)	225 g
4-oz. can	mushroom pieces	120 g
½ c.	green pepper (sliced)	125 mL
1 T.	parsley	15 mL
1 t.	garlic powder	5 mL
	salt and pepper to taste	
3 c.	mostaccioli noodles (cooked)	750 mL

Combine minced oysters with liquid, mushrooms, green pepper, and parsley in saucepan. Add garlic powder. Cook until green pepper is crispy tender. Add salt and pepper. Serve over mostaccioli noodles.

Microwave: Combine minced oysters with liquid, mushrooms, green pepper, parsley, and garlic powder in bowl. Cook on High for 4 minutes or until green pepper is crispy tender. Add salt and pepper. Serve over mostaccioli noodles.

Yield: 2 servings
Exchange 1 serving: 4 lean meat
1½ bread
Calories 1 serving: 195

Fish Noodle Special

¼ c.	condensed cream of celery soup	60 mL
2 T.	water	30 mL
2 T.	mushroom pieces	30 mL
2 T.	onion (finely chopped)	30 mL
dash each	thyme, ground rosemary, salt, pepper	dash each
1 c.	noodles (cooked)	250 mL
2 T.	peas	30 mL
3 oz.	cooked perch (flaked)	90 g

Blend condensed soup with water. Add mushrooms, onion, and seasonings; mix thoroughly. Combine noodles, peas, and perch in small baking dish. Pour soup mixture over entire surface; toss to mix. Bake at 350° F (175° C) for 30 minutes.

Microwave: Cook on High for 5 to 6 minutes.

Yield: 1 serving
Exchange: 3 lean meat
2½ bread
Calories: 285

Veal Steak Parmesan

1 T.	flour	15 mL
1 t.	salt	5 mL
dash each	poultry seasoning, salt, pepper, paprika	dash each
4 oz.	veal steak (cut in half)	120 g
1 t.	shortening	5 mL
½ c.	wide noodles (cooked)	125 mL
½ c.	Sour Cream Sauce, prepared	125 mL
3 T.	hot water	45 mL
1 t.	Parmesan cheese	5 mL

Combine flour, salt, and seasonings in shaker bag. Add veal steak; shake to coat. Remove veal from bag and shake off excess flour. Heat shortening in small skillet. Brown veal on both sides; place in small baking dish. Cover with noodles. Blend Sour Cream Sauce and hot water. Pour over noodles. Top with Parmesan cheese. Bake at 350° F (175° C) for 45 minutes, or until veal is tender.

Microwave: Cover. Cook on Medium to High for 15 minutes, or until meat is tender.

Yield: 1 serving
Exchange: 4¼ medium-fat meat
2 bread
Calories: 390

Kole 'n Klump

½ c.	Brussels sprouts	125 mL
2 oz.	lean pork cubes	60 g
pinch	caraway seeds, salt, pepper	pinch
¼ c.	potato (grated)	60 mL
¼ t.	onion salt	1 mL
dash each	thyme, salt, pepper	dash each

Boil Brussels sprouts, pork, caraway seeds, salt, and pepper with a small amount of water until partially cooked; drain. Place in individual baking dish. Cover with potato; sprinkle with onion salt, thyme, salt, and pepper. Cover tightly. Bake at 375 F (190° C) for 1 hour.

Microwave: Cook on High for 10 to 12 minutes. Turn dish a quarter turn after 6 minutes.

Yield: 1 serving
Exchange: 1 bread
2 high-fat meat
Calories: 232

Ham and Scalloped Potatoes

2 oz.	lean ham (diced)	60 g
1 medium	potato (peeled and sliced)	1 medium
2 T.	onion	30 mL
2 t.	parsley	10 mL
	vegetable cooking spray	
¼ c.	condensed cream of celery soup	60 mL
¼ c.	milk	60 mL
	salt and pepper to taste	

Combine ham, potato, onion, and parsley in baking dish coated with vegetable cooking spray. Blend condensed soup and milk; pour over potato mixture; cover. Bake at 350° F (175° C) for 1 hour, or until potatoes are tender. Add salt and pepper.

Microwave: Cook on high for 10 minutes, or until potatoes are tender. Add salt and pepper.

Yield: 1 serving
Exchange: 2 high-fat meat
1½ bread
½ milk
Calories: 365

Tuna Soufflé

11-oz. can	condensed cream of celery soup	300-g can
2 t.	parsley (finely chopped)	10 mL
1 t.	salt	5 mL
dash	pepper	dash
½ t.	marjoram	3 mL
7-oz. can	tuna (in water)	200-g can
6	eggs (separated)	6
1 c.	mixed vegetables (cooked)	250 mL

Combine condensed soup, parsley, salt, pepper, marjoram, and tuna in saucepan. Heat, stirring constantly, until mixture is hot. Remove from heat and cool slightly. Add egg yolks, one at a time, beating well after each addition. Stir in vegetables. Beat egg whites until soft peaks form. Fold small amount of beaten egg whites into egg yolk mixture, then fold egg yolk mixture into remaining egg whites. Pour into lightly greased 10-in. (25-cm) soufflé dish. Bake at 325° F (165° C) for 50 minutes, or until firm and golden brown. Serve immediately.

Yield: 8 servings
Exchange 1 serving: 1½ lean meat
1 bread
Calories 1 serving: 134

Hot Tuna Dish

½ c.	condensed cream of chicken soup	125 mL
2 oz.	chunk tuna (in water)	60 g
2 T.	celery (diced)	30 mL
1 T.	onion (chopped)	15 mL
1	egg (hard cooked)	1
4 T.	potato chips (crushed)	60 mL

Combine condensed soup, tuna, celery, and onion; mix thoroughly. Pour into small casserole. Slice egg; layer egg, then crushed potato chips. Bake at 350° F (175° C) for 20 minutes.

Microwave: Cook on Medium for 7 to 10 minutes.

Yield: 1 serving
Exchange: 1⅓ bread
3 medium-fat meat
Calories: 297

Casserole of Shrimp

2 t.	margarine	30 mL
1 T.	parsley (chopped)	15 mL
1 T.	sherry	15 mL
dash each	garlic powder, paprika, cayenne	dash each
½ c.	soft bread crumbs	125 mL
3 oz.	large shrimp (cooked)	90 g

Melt margarine over low heat. Add parsley, sherry, and seasonings; cook slightly. Add bread crumbs; toss to mix. Place shrimp in small baking dish. Top with bread crumb mixture. Bake at 325° F (165° C) for 20 minutes.

Microwave: Melt margarine; add parsley, sherry, and seasonings. Cook on High for 2 minutes. Add bread crumbs; toss to mix. Place shrimp in small baking dish. Top with bread crumb mixture. Cook on Medium for 5 to 7 minutes.

Yield: 1 serving
Exchange: 3 high-fat meat
1 bread
Calories: 204

Stuffed Cabbage Rolls

2 large	cabbage leaves	2 large
2 oz.	ground veal	60 g
2 oz.	ground lean beef	60 g
3 T.	skim milk	45 mL
1 slice	dry bread (crumbled)	1 slice
1 t.	onion (grated)	5 mL
dash each	salt, pepper, nutmeg	dash each
½ c.	beef broth	125 mL
1 T.	flour	15 mL

Cook cabbage leaves in boiling salted water until tender; drain. Combine ground veal, beef, skim milk, bread crumbs, onion, salt, pepper, and nutmeg; mix thoroughly. Place half of meat mixture in a cabbage leaf and roll up, tucking ends in. Secure with toothpicks. Place in small baking dish. Repeat with remaining meat mixture and cabbage leaf. Blend beef broth and flour; pour over cabbage rolls. Bake at 350° F (175° C) for 45 to 50 minutes.

Microwave: Cook on Medium for 10 to 12 minutes.

Yield: 1 serving
Exchange: 4 medium-fat meat
1 vegetable
1 bread
Calories: 396

Hungarian Goulash

1 T.	shortening or margarine	30 mL
1 oz.	lean beef (diced)	30 g
1 oz.	lean veal (diced)	30 g
1 oz.	beef kidney (diced)	30 g
2 t.	onion (chopped)	10 mL
1 t.	green pepper (chopped)	5 mL
3	cherry tomatoes (halved)	3
½ c.	potato (diced)	125 mL
¼ c.	carrot (diced)	60 mL
¼ t.	salt	1 mL
dash each	paprika, pepper, marjoram	dash each

Heat shortening or margarine in skillet; add meat. Brown on all sides; drain. Place in individual casserole. Add remaining ingredients. Add enough water to cover. Cover casserole tightly; bake at 350° F (175° C) for 1 hour.

Microwave: Cook on high for 20 to 25 minutes. Stir halfway through cooking time.

Yield: 1 serving
Exchange: 3 high-fat meat
1 bread
1 vegetable
Calories: 348

MEATS AND POULTRY

Steak Roberto

¼ c.	margarine	60 mL
1 t.	garlic powder	5 mL
1 lb.	beef tenderloin (8 slices)	500 g
½ t.	steak sauce	3 mL
¼ t.	bay leaf (crushed)	1 mL
1 T.	lemon juice	15 mL
½ t.	salt	2 mL
dash	pepper	dash

Melt margarine and combine with garlic powder. Set aside for 20 minutes to allow flavor to develop. Heat 1 T. (15 mL) of the garlic margarine in heavy skillet until very hot. Place as many beef tenderloin slices as possible in skillet; brown on both sides. Remove to warm steak platter. Repeat with remaining beef, if necessary. Reduce heat. Add remaining garlic margarine to pan. Add steak sauce, bay leaf, lemon juice, salt, and pepper; blend thoroughly. Pour over beef tenderloin on platter.

Yield: 8 servings
Exchange 1 serving: 2 medium-fat meat
½ fat
Calories 1 serving: 155

Brisket of Beef with Horseradish

3 to 4 lb.	beef brisket	1½ to 2 kg
	salt and pepper to taste	
1 medium	onion (sliced)	1 medium
1	bay leaf	1
1 T.	lemon juice	15 mL
½ c.	horseradish (grated)	125 mL
	salt and pepper to taste	

Place brisket in large kettle; add salt and pepper. Add onion, bay leaf, and enough water to cover brisket. Bring to a boil. Reduce heat and simmer for 2 hours. Remove brisket from water. Combine lemon juice and horseradish. Rub surface of brisket with horseradish mixture. Return brisket to kettle; cover. Cook 1 hour longer.

Exchange 1 oz. (30 g): 1 medium-fat meat
Calories 1 oz. (30 g): 84

Beef Fondue

1 small	tomato	1 small
2 c.	beef broth	500 mL
1	bay leaf	1
½ t.	rosemary (ground)	2 mL
	sirloin steak (cut into bite-size cubes)	

Peel and crush tomato. Place beef broth, tomato, bay leaf, and rosemary in saucepan; heat to a boil. Pour into fondue pot, keep hot with a burner. Place steak cubes on spear. Cook in hot broth to desired doneness.

Exchange 1 oz. (30 g): 1 high-fat meat
Calories 1 oz. (30 g): 88

NOTE: Amount of steak used depends on number of servings required.

Sauerbraten

4 oz.	lean beef roast	120 g
½ c.	beef broth	125 mL
¼ c.	water	60 mL
¼ c.	cider vinegar	60 mL
¼ t.	salt	1 mL
dash	garlic powder	dash
1 t.	margarine	5 mL

Place beef in glass pan or bowl. Combine remaining ingredients, except margarine; pour over beef. Marinate 4 to 5 days in refrigerator. Turn beef at least once a day. Melt margarine in small skillet; add beef and brown. Reduce heat. Add half of the marinade to the skillet. Simmer until beef is tender.

Yield: 1 serving
Exchange: 4 medium-fat meat
Calories: 300

Mushroom-Stuffed Pork Chops

2 T.	mushroom pieces	30 mL
1 t.	onion (chopped)	5 mL
½ t.	parsley (chopped)	2 mL
1 t.	raisins (soaked)	5 mL
¼ t.	nutmeg	1 mL
1	double pork chop	1

Combine ingredients for stuffing; stir to blend. Split meaty part of chop down to bone; do not split through bone. Fill with stuffing; secure with poultry pins. Place on baking sheet. Bake uncovered at 350° F (175° C) for 35 to 40 minutes, or until tender. Turn once.

Yield: 1 chop
Exchange 1 oz. (30 g): 1 high-fat meat
Calories 1 oz. (30 g):   109

Teriyaki Pork Steak

	pork steak (thinly sliced)	
½ c.	soy sauce	125 mL
1 T.	wine vinegar	15 mL
2 T.	lemon juice	30 mL
¼ c.	water	60 mL
2 T.	sugar replacement	30 mL
1½ t.	ginger	7 mL
½ t.	garlic powder	2 mL

Place slices of pork steak in shallow dish. Combine remaining ingredients; pour over pork. Marinate 1 to 2 hours; turn once. Broil pork 5 to 6 inches (12 to 15 cm) from heat, for 2-3 minutes per side. Turn and broil second side.

Exchange 1 oz. (30 g): 1 medium-fat meat
Calories 1 oz. (30 g): 89

NOTE: Amount of steak used depends on number of servings required.

Calf's Liver

1 T.	flour	15 mL
½ t.	bay leaf (finely crushed)	2 mL
¼ t.	nutmeg	1 mL
	salt and pepper to taste	
½ c.	beef broth	125 mL
3 oz.	calf's liver	90 g
	vegetable cooking spray	

Combine flour, bay leaf, nutmeg, salt, and pepper in shaker bag. Add liver; shake to coat. Remove liver from bag and shake off excess flour. Brown liver in heavy skillet coated with vegetable cooking spray. Reduce heat. Add beef broth; cover. Simmer for 25 to 30 minutes, or until tender.

Yield: 1 serving
Exchange: 3 lean meat
Calories: 132

56

Calf's Brains

1	calf's brain (trimmed)	1
2 T.	lemon juice	30 mL
1 T.	cider vinegar	15 mL
1 t.	thyme	5 mL
1	bay leaf	1
⅓ c.	onion (chopped)	90 mL
1	parsley sprig (chopped)	1
⅓ c.	celery (chopped)	90 mL

Rinse brain thoroughly. Cover with water. Add lemon juice and marinate for 2 to 4 hours. Drain. Cover with cold water. Add remaining ingredients. Bring to boil. Cover and simmer for 20 to 25 minutes, or until thoroughly cooked. Remove from heat. Allow to rest 15 minutes. Remove brain from water. Slice thin.

Yield: 1 brain
Exchange 1 oz. (30 g): 1 lean meat
Calories 1 oz. (30 g): 45

Veal Roast

2 to 3 lb.	veal roast	1 to 1½ kg
2 c.	beef broth	500 mL
1 medium	onion (sliced)	1 medium
1	bay leaf	1
¼ t.	thyme	1 mL
	salt and pepper to taste	

Place roast in heavy kettle or roasting pan. Combine remaining ingredients. Pour over roast. Bake at 375° F (190° C) for 2 to 2½ hours, or until meat is very tender. While baking, baste with pan juices.

Exchange 1 oz. (30 g): 1 lean meat
Calories 1 oz. (30 g): 55

Veal Scaloppine

2 oz.	veal steak (boned)	60 g
¼ c.	tomato (sieved)	60 mL
2 T.	green pepper (chopped)	30 mL
1 T.	mushroom pieces	15 mL
1 T.	onions (chopped)	15 mL
¼ t.	parsley	1 mL
dash each	garlic powder, oregano	dash each
	salt and pepper to taste	

Place veal on bottom of individual baking dish. Add remaining ingredients; cover. Bake at 350° F (175° C) for 45 minutes, or until meat is tender.

Microwave: Cook on High for 10 to 12 minutes. Turn and uncover last 2 minutes.

Yield: 1 serving
Exchange: 2 lean meat
1 vegetable
Calories: 164

Veal Scaloppine II

½ t.	margarine	3 mL
2 oz.	veal round steak (thinly sliced)	60 g
2 T.	tomato paste	30 mL
6 T.	water	90 mL
dash each	salt, pepper, oregano, garlic powder	dash each
1 T.	mushrooms (sliced)	15 mL
1 t.	onion (chopped)	5 mL
1 c.	spaghetti (cooked)	250 mL

Melt margarine in small skillet. Brown both sides of slices of veal steak. Place in small baking dish. Blend tomato paste, water, seasonings, mushrooms, and onion together. Pour over veal; cover. Bake at 350° F (175° C) for 30 minutes. Place veal on top of spaghetti. Pour sauce over all.

Microwave: Cook covered on Medium for 12 minutes.

Yield: 1 serving
Exchange: 2 medium-fat meat
2 bread
Calories: 310

Veal Roll

1 oz.	veal (thin slice)	30 g
	salt and pepper to taste	
½ oz.	prosciutto (thin slice)	15 g
½ oz.	Swiss cheese (thin slice)	15 g
	vegetable cooking spray	

Pound veal slice with mallet or edge of plate until very thin. Add salt and pepper. Place prosciutto on top and roll up. Secure with poultry pin. Brown in heavy skillet coated with vegetable cooking spray. Top with cheese slice. Cover. Cook over low heat just until cheese melts slightly. Serve on hot plate.

Yield: 1 serving
Exchange: 2 medium-fat meat
Calories: 156

Beef Tongue

1	beef tongue	1

Place tongue in large kettle; cover with water. Add 1 t. (5 mL) salt per qt. (L) of water. Bring to boil; reduce heat and simmer 3½ to 4 hours. Remove tongue; immediately place in ice water. Allow to soak 5 minutes. Remove skin and trim. Slice thin. Use for sandwiches.

Exchange 1 oz. (30 g): 1 lean meat
Calories 1 oz. (30 g): 51

Meat Loaf

2 lb.	lean ground beef	1 kg
¼ c.	onion (grated)	60 mL
1 c.	soft bread crumbs	250 mL
1	egg	1
¼ c.	parsley (finely snipped)	60 mL
1¼ t.	salt	6 mL
dash each	pepper, thyme, marjoram	dash each
1 t.	evaporated milk	5 mL

Combine all ingredients. Add just enough water to form firm ball. Press into baking dish. Bake at 350° F (175° C) for 1½ hours.

Microwave: Cook on High for 15 minutes. Turn dish halfway through cooking time. Allow to rest for 5 minutes before serving.

Yield: 12 servings
Exchange 1 serving: 2½ high-fat meat
    ¼ bread
Calories 1 serving: 237

Klip Klops

4 slices	bread (crust removed)	4 slices
½ c.	skim milk	125 mL
½ t.	garlic powder	2 mL
1 t.	onion salt	5 mL
1 lb.	lean ground beef	500 g
1	egg (beaten)	1
1 qt.	water	1 l
1 small	bay leaf	1 small
1 t.	salt	5 mL
1	clove	1

Soak bread in skim milk. Add garlic powder, onion salt,

ground beef, and egg; mix thoroughly. Form into 8 balls. Combine water, bay leaf, salt, and clove. Bring to boil. Drop balls into boiling water. Cook until beef is done (about 15 minutes). Drain before placing on hot platter.

Yield: 8 servings
Exchange 1 serving: 2 high-fat meat
1 bread
Calories 1 serving: 190

Roast Leg of Lamb

5 to 6 lb.	leg of lamb	2½ to 3 kg
½ c.	lo-cal Italian dressing	125 mL
½ c.	water	125 mL
3 T.	lemon juice	45 mL
1 t.	garlic powder	5 mL
½ t.	rosemary (ground)	2 mL
½ t.	thyme	2 mL
½ t.	mace	2 mL
1 t.	salt	5 mL
¼ t.	pepper	1 mL

Wipe lamb with damp cloth. Puncture lamb with long sharp spear or poultry pin. Place on a rack in roasting pan, fat side up. Blend remaining ingredients; pour over lamb. Roast uncovered at 325° F (165° C) for 3 to 3½ hours. Baste with pan juices every ½ hour. Add more Italian dressing and water, if necessary.

Exchange 1 oz. (30 g): 1 medium-fat meat
Calories 1 oz. (30 g): 75

Steak Hawaiian

3 oz.	beef top round steak (sliced)	90 g
½ t.	mace	2 mL
2 T.	unsweetened pineapple juice	30 mL
1	pineapple slice (unsweetened)	1

Pound slices of round steak with mallet or edge of plate until thin. Sprinkle both sides with mace. Place in aluminum foil. Sprinkle with pineapple juice; top with pineapple slice. Secure foil tightly. Place in baking dish. Bake at 350° F (175° C) for 40 to 45 minutes.

Microwave: Place in plastic wrap. Cook on High for 10 to 12 minutes.

Yield: 1 serving
Exchange: 3 lean meat
1 fruit
Calories: 200

Lamb Shish Kebab

4 lb.	lean lamb	2 kg
3	garlic cloves (crushed)	3
1½ t.	salt	7 mL
1	bay leaf	1
½ t.	pepper	3 mL
½ t.	ground allspice	3 mL
½ t.	ground clove	3 mL
1 t.	white vinegar	5 mL
1 c.	skim milk	250 mL

Cut lamb into 2-in. (5-cm) cubes. Combine remaining ingredients; blend thoroughly. Pour over lamb in large bowl; cover. Refrigerate overnight. Place lamb pieces on skewers. Barbecue or broil 10 to 15 minutes. Turn once.

Exchange 1 oz. (30 g): 1 medium-fat meat
Calories 1 oz. (30 g): 89

Swiss Steak

1 t.	margarine	5 mL
3 oz.	beef minute steak	90 g
	salt and pepper to taste	
¼ c.	celery (sliced)	60 mL
1 T.	onion (chopped)	15 mL
¼ c.	tomato (crushed)	60 mL
¼ c.	water	60 mL

Heat margarine until very hot. Salt and pepper the steak. Brown both sides; drain. Place in individual baking dish. Add salt, pepper, and remaining ingredients. Cover. Bake at 375° F (175° C) for 1 hour, or until steak is tender.

Microwave: Cook on High 8 to 10 minutes. Uncover last minute.

Yield: 1 serving
Exchange: 3 medium-fat meat
1 fat
Calories: 220

Roast Duck with Orange Sauce

4 to 5 lb.	duck	2 to 3 kg
2 medium	oranges	2 medium
	salt to taste	
	Orange Sauce (p. 134)	

Wash inside and outside of duck thoroughly. Remove any fat from tail or neck opening. Salt interior of bird. Cut each orange (with peel) into 8 sections. Place inside of duck. Secure tail and neck skin, legs and wings with poultry pins. Salt exterior of duck. Place breast side up on a rack in roasting pan. Bake at 350° F (175° C) for 4 hours. During the final hour, baste with Orange Sauce every 15 minutes.

Exchange 1 oz. (30 g): 1 high-fat meat
Calories 1 oz. (30 g): 96

Roast Goose

5 to 6 lb.	goose	2½ to 3 kg
	salt to taste	

Wash and dry goose thoroughly. Salt cavity and exterior. Fill cavity loosely with stuffing. Close cavity and secure tightly. Place breast side up in roasting pan. Roast at 350° F (175° C) for 30 to 40 minutes per pound, or about 3 to 4 hours. Cover with a loose tent of aluminum foil for the last hour to prevent excess browning.

Yield: 8 to 10 servings
Exchange 1 oz. (30 g): 1 high-fat meat (without skin)
Calories 1 oz. (30 g): 120 (without skin)

NOTE: Add exchanges and calories for Stuffing.

Pollo Lesso

3 oz.	chicken breast (boned)	90 g
½	tomato (cut in 4 pieces)	½
¼	cucumber (peeled and sliced)	¼
¼ c.	peas	60 mL
dash each	salt, pepper, parsley	dash each

Remove skin from chicken breast; boil chicken in small amount of salted water until almost tender. Add tomato pieces, cucumber slices, and peas. Heat thoroughly; drain. Place on serving plate. Sprinkle with salt, pepper, and parsley.

Microwave: Place skinned chicken breast in individual dish; cover with plastic wrap. Cook on High for 12 minutes. Drain off any moisture. Add vegetables. Sprinkle with salt, pepper, and parsley. Cook on Medium for 4 minutes.

Yield: 1 serving
Exchange: 3 lean meat
1 bread
Calories: 202

Giblet-Stuffed Chicken

2	giblets	2
1 t.	margarine	5 mL
2 T.	rice	30 mL
1 T.	raisins	15 mL
1 T.	unsalted peanuts	15 mL
	salt and pepper to taste	
3 oz.	chicken breast (skinned and boned)	90 g

Simmer giblets in boiling water for 1 hour, or until tender. Drain. Remove tough center core from giblets. Chop giblets into small pieces. Melt margarine in small skillet. Sauté rice, raisins, giblets, and peanuts until rice and giblets are golden brown. Remove from heat. Add salt and pepper. Add ¼ c. (60 mL) water. Cover and return to heat. Simmer for 15 minutes or until water is absorbed. Remove from heat. Remove cover and allow to cool slightly. Place chicken breast, boned side up between two sheets of plastic wrap or waxed paper. Pound from center with the heel of your hand or edge of a plate to flatten. Place dressing in center. Fold over and secure with toothpicks or poultry pins. Place in small baking dish. Bake in preheated oven at 350° F (175° C) for 1 hour, or until golden brown.

Microwave: Sprinkle with paprika and parsley. Cook on High for 18 minutes.

Yield: 1 serving
Exchange: 3½ lean meat
½ fruit
¼ bread
1½ fat
Calories: 255

El Dorado

½ c.	chicken broth	125 mL
½ oz.	fresh oysters	15 g
1 t.	margarine	5 mL
1 T.	carrot (grated)	15 mL
2 T.	celery (chopped)	30 mL
1 t.	parsley (chopped)	5 mL
1 oz.	cooked chicken (diced)	30 g
	salt and pepper to taste	

Heat chicken broth to a boil; add oysters. Cook until edges roll; drain. Heat margarine in heavy skillet. Add carrot, celery, and parsley. Sauté until crisp-tender. Add chicken, oysters, and 1 T. (15 mL) of the chicken broth. Cook until thoroughly heated. Drain, if necessary. Add salt and pepper.

Yield: 1 serving
Exchange: 1½ lean meat
2 fat
Calories: 80

Chicken Livers

3 oz.	chicken livers	90 g
½ c.	skim milk	125 mL
2 T.	flour	30 mL
	salt and pepper to taste	
2 t.	margarine	10 mL

Soak chicken livers in skim milk overnight. Drain. Combine flour, salt, and pepper in shaker bag. Add livers, one at a time; shake to coat. Remove livers from bag and shake off excess flour. Melt margarine in small skillet; add livers. Cook until lightly browned and tender.

Yield: 1 serving
Exchange: 3 lean meat
2 fat
Calories: 190

FISH, SEAFOOD, AND EGGS

Fish Florentine

2 T.	onion (chopped)	30 mL
½ c.	mushrooms (chopped)	125 mL
1 T.	margarine	15 mL
2 c.	cooked spinach (well drained)	500 mL
1 t.	lemon juice	5 mL
1 c.	White Sauce (p. 134)	250 mL
3 oz.	Cheddar cheese (grated)	90 g
12 oz.	cooked fish (flaked)	360 g

Sauté onion and mushrooms in margarine until onion is transparent. Add spinach and lemon juice; mix well. Pour into baking dish or 6 individual baking dishes coated with vegetable cooking spray. Cover with ½ c. (125 mL) of the White Sauce. Sprinkle with 1½ oz. (45 mL) of the cheese. Cover with fish, then with remaining sauce. Sprinkle with remaining cheese. Bake at 350° F (175° C) for 20 minutes.

Microwave: Cook on Medium for 10 minutes; turn. Cook 5 minutes more. Hold 3 minutes.

Yield:	6 servings
Exchange 1 serving:	3½ high-fat meat
	1 vegetable
	1 bread
	½ milk
	1 fat
Calories 1 serving:	215

NOTE: Yield is not listed for some recipes where some people are allowed 1 exchange while others are allowed 2 or more.

Poached Fish

2 lb.	fish (haddock, cod, pollack, salmon)	1 kg
1 qt.	water	1 L
1	carrot (sliced)	1
1	onion (sliced)	1
1	bay leaf	1
½ t.	thyme	3 mL
½ t.	whole peppercorns	3 mL

Wash fish; wrap in cheesecloth. Combine remaining ingredients in large kettle. Bring to a boil; reduce heat and cook for 15 minutes. Add fish and cook at a simmer. Time depends on thickness, not weight; cook 10 minutes for each in. (2.5 cm) of thickness. Drain in cheesecloth. Turn out onto warm serving platter. Remove skin carefully.

Exchange 1 oz. (30 g): 1 meat
Calories 1 oz. (30 g): 21

NOTE: Bone is not counted in serving weight.

Broiled Trout

5 oz.	trout fillet	150 g
1 t.	margarine	5 mL
dash each	lemon, pepper, marjoram, salt, paprika	dash each

Clean trout fillet thoroughly; pat dry. Melt margarine; brush on both sides of fillet. Sprinkle with seasonings in order given. Broil 5 to 6 in. (12 to 15 cm) from heat for 10 to 15 minutes. It is not necessary to turn the fillet.

Yield: 1 serving
Exchange: 5 lean meat
1 fat
Calories: 190

Broiled Smelt

3 oz.	smelt	90 g
	salt and pepper to taste	
1 t.	margarine	5 mL
1 t.	lemon juice	5 mL

Dry smelt thoroughly. Salt and pepper cavity of smelt. Melt margarine; brush on both sides of smelt. Sprinkle with lemon juice. Add salt and pepper. Broil 6 to 8 in. (15 to 20 cm) from heat for 10 to 15 minutes.

Yield: 1 serving
Exchange: 3 medium-fat meat
Calories: 95

Baked White Fish

1 t.	margarine	5 mL
3 oz.	white fish fillet	90 g
	salt and pepper to taste	

Melt margarine; brush on both sides of fish fillet. Place fish on aluminum foil. Add salt and pepper. Wrap tightly, securing ends. Place on baking sheet. Bake at 375° F (190° C) for 45 minutes.

Microwave: Wrap in plastic wrap; prick wrap. Place on cooking rack. Cook for 7 to 8 minutes, giving package a quarter turn after 4 minutes.

Yield: 1 serving
Exchange: 3 medium-fat meat
　　　　　　　 1 fat
Calories: 229

Mustard Halibut Steaks

3 oz.	halibut steak	90 g
1 t.	margarine	5 mL
1 t.	lemon juice	5 mL
½ t.	Dijon mustard	3 mL
dash each	lemon rind, sugar replacement	dash each
	salt to taste	

Wash and dry halibut thoroughly. Melt margarine; brush on both sides of halibut. Lay on broiler pan. Brush top with mixture of lemon juice, Dijon mustard, and seasonings. Broil 5 to 6 in. (12 to 15 cm) from heat for 3 to 4 minutes. Turn halibut; repeat on second side.

Yield: 1 serving
Exchange: 1 lean meat
1 fat
Calories: 90

Fish Creole

2 lb.	whitefish fillets	1 kg
3 c.	water	750 mL
1	bay leaf	1
3 stalks	celery with tops (chopped)	3 stalks
	salt and pepper to taste	
2 c.	Creole Sauce (p. 128)	500 mL

Cut fish into serving pieces. Combine water, bay leaf, celery, salt, and pepper in saucepan. Boil for 2 to 3 minutes. Remove from heat. Add fish pieces and allow water to cool completely. Drain fish and celery; remove bay leaf. Heat Creole Sauce. Add fish and celery. Simmer on low heat for 5 minutes.

Yield: 6 servings
Exchange one serving: 5 medium-fat meat
Calories one serving: 370

Individual Mackerel

3 oz.	cooked mackerel (flaked)	90 g
2 T.	mushrooms (chopped)	30 mL
1 t.	onion (finely chopped)	5 mL
1 t.	celery (finely chopped)	5 mL
½ slice	bread (crumbled)	½ slice
½ t.	parsley (finely chopped)	3 mL
1	egg (beaten)	1
1 t.	ketchup	5 mL
	salt and pepper to taste	

Combine all ingredients. Mix thoroughly. Place in small baking dish. Bake at 350° F (175° C) for 40 minutes.

Microwave: Cook on Medium for 10 to 12 minutes.

Yield: 1 serving
Exchange: 4 medium-fat meat
½ bread
Calories: 322

Baked Turbot

4 oz.	turbot fillet	120 g
1 t.	margarine	5 mL
1 t.	lemon juice	5 mL
dash each	salt, pepper, paprika, parsley	dash each

Clean turbot fillet thoroughly; pat dry. Melt margarine; brush on both sides of fillet. Place on aluminum foil. Sprinkle with lemon juice, then seasonings. Wrap up fillet securely; lay in cake pan. Bake at 350° F (175° C) for 30 to 40 minutes. Slide fish out of foil onto warm serving plate.

Yield: 1 serving
Exchange: 4 medium-fat meat
1 fat
Calories: 400

Salmon Loaf

16 oz.	cooked salmon (flaked)	500 g
2 T.	onion (chopped)	30 mL
3 T.	vegetable juice	45 mL
¼ t.	marjoram	2 mL
2	eggs	2
1 c.	bread crumbs (finely ground)	250 mL
	salt and pepper to taste	

If canned salmon is used, drain thoroughly. Combine with remaining ingredients. Blend thoroughly. Allow to rest for 5 minutes, or until bread crumbs are soft. Blend again. Line a 9 x 5-in. (23 x 13-cm) loaf pan with waxed paper. Pack salmon mixture tightly into loaf pan. Bake at 350° F (175° C) for 40 minutes.

Yield: 6 servings
Exchange 1 serving: 3 medium-fat meat
½ bread
Calories 1 serving: 255

Cooked Flaked Fish

| 1 lb. | any raw fish | 500 g |

Clean fish and cook in salted boiling water for 15 to 20 minutes. Remove skin and bones. Flake fish.

Exchange 1 oz. (30 g) serving: 1 meat
Calories 1 oz. (30 g) serving: 25

Finnan Haddie

3 oz.	cooked finnan haddie	90 g
1 T.	leek (chopped)	15 mL
1 T.	green pepper (chopped)	15 mL
2 t.	pimientos (chopped)	10 mL
¼ c.	condensed cream of mushroom soup	60 mL
	salt and pepper to taste	
½ oz.	Cheddar cheese (grated)	15 g

Arrange finnan haddie in baking dish. Combine leek, green pepper, pimientos, and condensed soup. Stir to mix. Add salt and pepper. Pour over fish. Top with cheese. Bake at 350° F (175° C) for 20 to 25 minutes.

Microwave: Cook on Medium for 10 minutes. Turn once.

Yield: 1 serving
Exchange: 3½ medium-fat meat
½ bread
1 fat
Calories: 220

Great Crab

1 t.	butter	5 mL
dash each	lemon juice, parsley, rosemary, salt, paprika	dash each
2 oz.	crabmeat	60 g

Melt butter in small saucepan. Mix in lemon juice and seasonings. Add crabmeat. Toss to coat and heat.

Yield: 1 serving
Exchange: 2 lean meat
1 fat
Calories: 100

Marinated Crab Legs

½ c.	Teriyaki Marinade (p. 134)	125 mL
⅓ c.	lemon juice	80 mL
½ c.	water	125 mL
1 t.	basil	5 mL
1 to 2 lb.	cooked crab legs, shelled	500 to 1000 g

Combine marinade, lemon juice, water, and basil. Add crab legs. (If necessary, add more water to cover legs.) Marinate 2 to 3 hours.

Exchange 1 oz. (30 g): 1 lean meat
Calories 1 oz. (30 g):   32

Oysters on the Shell

2 oz.	oysters	60 g
2 T.	mushroom pieces	30 mL
1 t.	onion (diced)	5 mL
¼ c.	vegetable broth	60 mL
1 slice	bread (finely crumbled)	1 slice
¼ t.	lemon juice	1 mL
	salt and pepper to taste	
1	oyster shell	1
¼ oz.	Cheddar cheese (grated)	8 g

Cook oysters in small amount of boiling salted water until edges start to curl. Drain (reserve some liquid). Combine mushrooms, onion, and broth in saucepan. Bring to a boil. Reduce heat. Add bread crumbs; stir to mix. Remove from heat. Add lemon juice and enough reserved oyster liquid to moisten bread-crumb mixture thoroughly. Add oysters, salt, and pepper. Heap into shell or small baking dish. Top with cheese. Broil until cheese melts.

Yield: 1 serving
Exchange: 2½ lean meat
              1 bread
Calories: 125

Clam Mousse

1 env.	unflavored gelatin	1 env.
1 cube	vegetable bouillon	1 cube
½ c.	boiling water	125 mL
8 oz.	minced clams (and juice)	240 g
8 oz.	yogurt	240 g
1 t.	lemon juice	5 mL
1 t.	celery flakes	5 mL
1 t.	parsley flakes	5 mL
	small dash cayenne	

Dissolve gelatin and bouillon cube in boiling water. Beat in remaining ingredients with whisk or electric mixer. Pour into mold and chill until firm.

Yield: 4 servings
Exchange 1 serving: 2 lean meat
¼ milk
Calories 1 serving: 70

Shrimp Soufflé

2 oz.	shrimp (canned)	60 g
dash each	thyme, rosemary (crushed), salt, pepper	dash each
1	egg, separated	1
	vegetable cooking spray	

Break shrimp into fine pieces. Add to beaten egg yolk and seasonings. Beat egg whites until stiff. Gently stir half of egg white into shrimp mixture. Gently fold in remaining egg white. Pour into large individual soufflé dish coated with vegetable cooking spray. (Dish should be less than two-thirds full.) Bake at 375° F (190° C) for 15 to 20 minutes.

Yield: 1 serving
Exchange: 3 lean meat
Calories: 205

Tomato Stuffed with Crab Louis

½ t.	ketchup	2 mL
1 t.	mayonnaise	5 mL
¼ t.	Worcestershire sauce	1 mL
1 oz.	crabmeat	30 g
1 t.	green onion (finely chopped)	5 mL
1 T.	celery (finely chopped)	15 mL
1 T.	green pepper (finely chopped)	15 mL
1 t.	parsley (finely chopped)	5 mL
3	almonds (chopped)	3
1	tomato (peeled)	1
1	lettuce leaf	1

To make Crab Louis, blend ketchup, mayonnaise, and Worcestershire sauce; add crabmeat, green onion, celery, green pepper, parsley, and almonds. Stir to bind; chill. Cut peeled tomato into 6 sections, slicing almost to the bottom. Fill with Crab Louis. Serve on lettuce leaf.

Yield: 1 serving
Exchange: 1 medium-fat meat
1 fat
1 vegetable
Calories: 110

Venetian Seafood

½ c.	water	125 mL
2 T.	lime juice	30 mL
1 T.	chives (finely chopped)	15 mL
1 t.	garlic powder	5 mL
½ t.	oregano	3 mL
½ t.	salt	3 mL
¼ t.	pepper	1 mL
1 oz.	fresh or frozen lobster (thawed and cubed)	30 g
1 oz.	fresh or frozen scallops (thawed)	30 g
1 oz.	fresh or frozen shrimp (thawed)	30 g
	vegetable cooking spray	

Make a marinade by blending water, lime juice, and seasonings. Place thawed seafood in deep narrow dish. Pour marinade over seafood to cover. Refrigerate for 3 to 5 hours. (Stir occasionally if seafood is not completely covered with marinade.) Drain. Spray seafood with vegetable cooking spray. Place on baking sheet or dish coated with vegetable cooking spray. Broil 5 to 6 in. (12 to 15 cm) from heat for 5-6 minutes until seafood is tender. Shake baking sheet or dish occasionally to brown seafood evenly.

Yield: 1 serving
Exchange: 3 lean meat
Calories: 90

Long Island Boil

1 oz.	mussels	30 g
1	tomato (peeled and quartered)	1
1	onion (cut into large chunks)	1
½ t.	garlic powder	2 mL
1 t.	parsley	5 mL
1 oz.	halibut (cut into chunks)	30 g
1 oz.	scallops	30 g
	salt and pepper to taste	

Wash mussels thoroughly. Soak in cold water overnight. Steam mussels until shells open; remove mussels from shells. Combine tomato, onion, garlic powder, and parsley. Simmer for 15 minutes. Add halibut and scallops. Cover; simmer 10 minutes. Add mussels, salt and pepper. Heat thoroughly.

Yield: 1 serving
Exchange: 3 lean meat
           1 vegetable
Calories: 105

Lobster Orientale

1 c.	chicken broth	250 mL
4	shallots	4
¼ t.	ginger	1 mL
¼ t.	curry powder	1 mL
1 oz.	pork (cubed)	30 g
2 oz.	lobster (cubed)	60 g
1 t.	cornstarch	5 mL
¼ c.	cold water	60 mL
½ c.	bean sprouts	125 mL

Combine chicken broth, shallots, ginger, and curry powder. Heat to a boil. Add pork; cook until tender. Remove from heat. Add lobster. Dissolve cornstarch in cold water. Combine with pork-lobster mixture. Return to heat; thicken slightly. Add bean sprouts. Heat thoroughly. (Add extra water if mixture thickens too much.)

Yield: 1 serving
Exchange: 3 medium-fat meat
Calories: 140

Shrimp Creole

½ c.	Creole Sauce (p. 128)	125 mL
10	small shrimp	10
1 c.	rice (cooked)	250 mL

Heat Creole Sauce just to a boil. Add shrimp. Remove from heat. Allow to rest 10 minutes. Serve over rice.

Yield: 1 serving
Exchange: 2 meat
2 bread
½ vegetable
1 fat
Calories: 238

Seafood Medley

1 oz.	chunk tuna	30 g
1 oz.	small shrimp (cooked)	30 g
1 t.	lemon juice	5 mL
½	egg (hard cooked and chopped)	½
1 t.	green onion (sliced)	5 mL
1	lettuce leaf	1

Combine all ingredients, except lettuce. Chill thoroughly before serving on lettuce leaf with favorite dressing.

Yield: 1 serving
Exchange: 2½ medium-fat meat
           ¼ vegetable
Calories: 137

Montana Eggs

1	egg (beaten)	1
½ oz.	ham (finely chopped)	15 g
1 t.	onion (finely chopped)	5 mL
	salt and pepper to taste	
	vegetable cooking spray	

Combine egg, ham, onion, salt, and pepper in small bowl. Beat to blend. Coat pan with vegetable cooking spray; heat to moderately hot. Add egg mixture. Cook on low heat; stir to scramble.

Yield: 1 serving
Exchange: 1½ high-fat meat
Calories: 125

Basic Omelet

vegetable cooking spray
1   egg (well beaten)   1
salt and pepper to taste

Coat pan with vegetable cooking spray; heat pan to moderately hot. Add beaten egg and cook over low heat. Lift edges of egg very carefully to allow uncooked portion of egg to run under. Add salt and pepper. When mixture is firm, fold omelet in half, or roll up jelly-roll style. A filling may be added before folding.

Yield: 1 omelet
Exchange: 1 medium-fat meat
Calories: 78

Omelet Fillings

Just before folding omelet, add one or more of the following:

Bean Sprout: ¼ c. (60 mL) bean sprouts

Broccoli: ¼ c. (60 mL) chopped broccoli

Cheese: 1 oz. (30 g) cheese (**Exchange:** 1 high-fat meat; **Calories:** 100)

Chicken Liver: 1 oz. (30 g) cooked chopped chicken livers (**Exchange:** 1 lean meat; **Calories:** 45)

Crab: 1 oz. (30 g) flaked crabmeat (**Exchange:** 1 lean meat; **Calories:** 25)

Dried Beef: 1 oz. (30 g) chopped dried beef (**Exchange:** 1 medium-fat meat; **Calories:** 80)

Green Pepper and Celery: 1 T. (15 mL) chopped green pepper, 1 T. (15 mL) chopped celery

Ham: 1 oz. (30 g) ham (**Exchange:** 1 high-fat meat; **Cal-ories:** 100)

Herb: 1 T. (15 mL) chopped parsley, 1 t. (5 mL) chives, dash thyme
(Add herbs to beaten egg before cooking.)

Mushroom: 1 T. (15 mL) mushroom pieces

Tomato: 2 T. (30 mL) chopped tomato flesh

Tuna: 1 oz. (30 g) drained, water-packed tuna (**Exchange:** 1 lean meat; **Calories:** 50)

NOTE: Where exchange and calories are listed for filling, these must be added to exchange and calories of omelet.

Eggs Florentine

	vegetable cooking spray	
2 T.	cooked spinach (chopped)	30 mL
1	egg	1
	salt and pepper to taste	
½ oz.	cheese (grated)	15 g

Spray individual baking dish with vegetable cooking spray. Cover bottom with spinach. Add egg, salt, and pepper. Top with cheese. Bake at 350° F (175° C) for 15 minutes, or until white is set.

Microwave: Prick egg yolk. Cover. Cook on High for 4 to 5 minutes.

Yield: 1 serving
Exchange: 1½ medium-fat meat
Calories: 140

Cottage Eggs

3	asparagus spears	3
1	egg	1
	salt and pepper to taste	
1 oz.	Swiss cheese (grated)	30 g

Steam asparagus spears until tender. Place in individual baking dish. Poach egg; add salt and pepper. Place on top of asparagus. Top with cheese. Broil until cheese melts.

Yield: 1 serving
Exchange: 2 high-fat meat
                    1 vegetable
Calories: 216

Eggs Benedict

half	English muffin	half
1 oz.	lean ham slice	30 g
1	egg	1
1 T.	Hollandaise Sauce (p. 133)	15 mL
	salt and pepper to taste	

Toast muffin half. Cook ham over low heat. Place on muffin. Poach egg and place on top of ham. Spoon Hollandaise Sauce over egg. Add salt and pepper.

Yield: 1 serving
Exchange: 2⅛ high-fat meat
                    ½ bread
                    1 fat
Calories: 266

BREADS

Bran Bread

3 T.	shortening	45 mL
3 T.	brown sugar replacement	45 mL
3 T.	molasses	45 mL
1 t.	salt	5 mL
½ c.	bran	125 mL
¾ c.	boiling water	190 mL
1 pkg.	dry yeast	1 pkg.
¼ c.	warm water	60 mL
2½ c.	flour	625 mL
	margarine (melted)	

Place shortening, brown sugar replacement, molasses, salt, and bran in large mixing bowl. Add boiling water. Stir to blend. Soften dry yeast in warm water. Allow to rest for 5 minutes. Add yeast to bran mixture. Add flour, 1 c. (250 mL) at a time, stirring well between additions, until a soft dough is formed. Knead gently for 10 minutes. Shape into loaf. Place in greased 13 x 9 x 2-in. (23 x 13 x 5-cm) loaf pan. Cover; allow to rise for 2 hours. Punch down; allow to rise for 1 hour. Bake at 325° F (165° C) for 50 to 55 minutes. Remove to rack and brush lightly with melted margarine.

Yield: 1 loaf (14 slices)
Exchange 1 slice: 1 bread
Calories 1 slice: 68

Jewish Braid Bread (Challah)

1 pkg.	dry yeast	1 pkg.
¾ c.	warm water	190 mL
1 t.	salt	5 mL
¼ c.	sugar replacement	60 mL
2 T.	margarine (melted)	30 mL
2	eggs (well beaten)	2
3 c.	flour	750 mL
1 t.	skim milk	5 mL
	poppy seeds	

Soften yeast in warm water; allow to rest for 5 minutes. Add salt, sugar replacement, and margarine. Measure 1 T. (15 mL) of the beaten eggs. Place in cup and reserve. Add remaining eggs and 1 c. (250 mL) of the flour to yeast mixture; beat vigorously. Add remaining flour. Turn onto floured board and knead until smooth and elastic. Place in lightly greased bowl; cover. Allow to rise until double in size, about 1½ hours. Punch down; divide into thirds. Roll into 3 strips, 18 in. (45 cm) long, with the heel of the hand. Braid the 3 strips loosely, tucking under ends. Blend reserved beaten egg with 1 t. (5 mL) skim milk, carefully brush over braid. Sprinkle with poppy seeds; cover. Allow to rise until double in size, about 1½ hours. Bake at 350° F (175° C) for 1 hour, or until done.

Yield: 1 loaf (18 slices)
Exchange 1 slice: 1 bread
Calories 1 slice: 70

Quick Onion Bread

1 loaf	frozen bread dough	1 loaf
1 pkg.	onion soup mix	1 pkg.

Allow bread to thaw as directed on package. Roll dough out on unfloured board. Sprinkle half of soup mix over surface. Roll up jelly-roll style. Knead to work mix into dough; repeat

with remaining soup mix. Form into loaf. Place in greased
9 x 5-in. (23 x 13-cm) loaf pan; cover. Allow to rise about 2
hours. Bake at 350° F (175° C) for 30 to 40 minutes, or until
done.

Yield: 1 loaf (14 slices)
Exchange 1 slice: 1 bread
Calories 1 slice: 80

Apricot Bread

8	dried apricot halves	8
⅓ c.	shortening	90 mL
¼ c. (packed)	brown sugar replacement	60 mL (packed)
2	eggs (beaten)	2
1 c.	skim milk	250 mL
½ t.	salt	2 mL
1½ t.	baking powder	7 mL
¼ t.	cinnamon	1 mL
dash	nutmeg	dash
¾ c.	flour	190 mL

Soak apricots in warm water for 2 hours. Cook over medium
heat for 10 minutes; drain and chop fine. Cream shortening
and brown sugar replacement. Add eggs and skim milk; beat
thoroughly. Add salt, baking powder, cinnamon, and nutmeg. Stir in apricots and enough of the flour to make a thick
cake batter. Pour into greased 9 x 5-in. (23 x 13-cm) loaf pan.
Bake at 350° F (175° C) for 1½ hours, or until toothpick
comes out clean.

Microwave: Bake on Low for 20 minutes. Increase heat to
High for 5 minutes, or until toothpick comes out clean. Hold
2 minutes. Turn pan a quarter turn every 10 minutes.

Yield: 1 loaf (14 slices)
Exchange 1 slice: 1 bread
                      1 fat
Calories 1 slice: 75

Raisin Bread

1 pkg.	dry yeast	1 pkg.
¼ c.	warm water	60 mL
¾ c.	milk (scalded and cooled)	180 mL
2 T.	sugar replacement	30 mL
1 t.	salt	5 mL
1	egg	1
2 T.	margarine (softened)	30 mL
3¾ c.	flour	940 mL
1 c.	raisins	250 mL

Soften yeast in warm water; allow to rest for 5 minutes. Combine milk, sugar replacement, salt, egg, and margarine; mix thoroughly. Stir in yeast mixture. Add 1 c. (250 mL) of the flour. Beat until smooth. Mix in raisins. Blend in remaining flour. Knead for 5 minutes. Cover; allow to rise for 2 hours. Punch down; form into loaf. Place in greased 9 x 5-in. (23 x 13-cm) loaf pan; cover. Allow to rise for 1 hour. Bake at 400° F (200° C) for 30 minutes, or until loaf sounds hollow and is golden brown. Remove to rack.

Yield: 1 loaf (14 slices)
Exchange 1 slice: 1 bread
Calories 1 slice: 68

Pita Bread

1 pkg.	dry yeast	1 pkg.
½ t.	sugar replacement	3 mL
1 t.	salt	5 mL
1 T.	liquid shortening	15 mL
1½ c.	warm water	375 mL
4 c.	flour	1000 mL

Dissolve yeast, sugar, salt, and liquid shortening in warm water. Add 3 c. (750 mL) of the flour; stir to mix well. (Dough should be fairly stiff; if not, add more flour.) Turn out onto floured surface; knead in remaining flour. (Dough will be very stiff.) Form into 15½-in. (40-cm) tube. Cut into 15 slices. Pat to make circles about 6 in. (15 cm) in diameter. Lay on lightly greased baking pans; cover. Allow to rise until almost doubled, about 1½–2 hours. Bake 475° F (245° C) for 10 to 12 minutes, or until lightly golden brown, puffed, and hollow. These freeze well.

Yield: 15 pita bread pockets
Exchange 1 pocket: 1½ bread
½ fat
Calories 1 pocket: 70

Pioneer Cornbread

1	egg	1
1 c.	skim milk	250 mL
2 T.	lo-cal maple syrup	30 mL
2 T.	margarine (melted)	30 mL
⅔ c.	cornmeal	160 mL
¾ c.	flour	190 mL
1 T.	baking powder	30 mL
1 t.	salt	5 mL

Beat egg until light and lemon colored. Add skim milk, maple syrup, and margarine. Combine cornmeal, flour, baking powder, and salt in large bowl. Stir to blend. Gradually add flour mixture to liquid. Pour into greased 8-in. (20-cm) square pan. Bake at 425° F (220° C) for 20 to 25 minutes.

Microwave: Bake on Low for 10 minutes. Increase heat to High for 5 minutes, or until toothpick comes out clean.

Yield: 9 squares
Exchange 1 square: 1½ bread
Calories 1 square: 82

Baking Powder Biscuits

1 c.	flour	250 mL
1 t.	baking powder	5 mL
¼ t.	yeast	2 mL
¼ t.	salt	2 mL
1 T.	liquid shortening	15 mL
6 T.	milk	90 mL
	vegetable cooking spray	

Combine all ingredients, except vegetable cooking spray; mix just until blended. Turn out on floured board. Roll out to a ½-in. (1-cm) thickness. Cut into circles with floured 2-in. (5-cm) cutter. Place on baking sheet coated with vegetable cooking spray; cover. Allow to rest for 10 minutes. Bake at 450° F (230° C) for 12 to 15 minutes, or until lightly browned.

Yield: 10 biscuits
Exchange 1 biscuit: 1 bread
½ fat
Calories 1 biscuit: 90

Yeast Rolls

1 pkg.	dry yeast	1 pkg.
¼ c.	warm water	60 mL
2 T.	sugar replacement	30 mL
2 t.	salt	10 mL
1 T.	margarine (melted)	15 mL
¾ c.	warm water	190 mL
3½ c.	flour	875 mL
1	egg (well beaten)	1

Soften yeast in the ¼ c. (60 mL) warm water. Allow to rest for 5 minutes. Combine sugar replacement, salt, margarine, and the ¾ c. (190 mL) warm water; stir to mix. Add 1 c. (250 mL) of the flour; beat well. Blend in yeast mixture and the egg. Add remaining flour; mix well. Knead gently until dough is smooth; cover. Allow to rise for 1 hour. Punch down. Allow to rest for 10 minutes. Shape into 36 rolls. Place on greased cookie sheet or in greased muffin tins. Allow to rise until doubled in size, about 1½–2 hours. Bake at 400° F (200° C) for 20 to 25 minutes, or until golden brown.

Yield: 36 rolls
Exchange 1 roll: 68
Calories 1 roll: 1 bread

Orange Muffins

1 c.	orange juice	250 mL
1 T.	orange peel (grated)	30 mL
½ c.	raisins (soaked)	125 mL
⅓ c.	sugar replacement	80 mL
1 T.	margarine	30 mL
1	egg	1
¼ t.	salt	2 mL
1 t.	baking soda	5 mL
1 t.	baking powder	5 mL
½ t.	vanilla extract	2 mL
2 c.	flour	500 mL

Combine orange juice, orange peel, and raisins. Allow to rest for 1 hour. Cream together the sugar replacement, margarine, and egg. Add salt, baking soda, baking powder, and vanilla extract. Stir in orange juice mixture. Stir in enough of the flour to make a thick cake batter. Spoon into greased muffin tins, filling no more than two-thirds full. Bake at 350° F (175° C) for 20 to 25 minutes, or until done.

Microwave: Spoon into 6-oz. (180-mL) custard cups, filling no more than two-thirds full. Cook on Low for 7 to 8 minutes. Increase heat to High for 2 minutes, or until done.

Yield: 24 muffins
Exchange 1 muffin: 1 bread
Calories 1 muffin: 68

Fresh Apple Muffins

2 T.	soft margarine	30 mL
2 T.	sugar replacement	30 mL
1	egg (beaten)	1
1¼ c.	flour	310 mL
¼ t.	salt	2 mL
2 t.	baking powder	10 mL
6 T.	skim milk	90 mL
1 small	apple (peeled and chopped)	1 small

Cream margarine and sugar replacement; add egg. Stir in remaining ingredients. Spoon into greased muffin tins, filling no more than two-thirds full. Bake at 400° F (200° C) for 25 minutes, or until done.

Yield: 12 muffins
Exchange 1 muffin: 1 bread
Calories 1 muffin: 72

Popovers

1 c.	flour	250 mL
½ t.	salt	3 mL
2	eggs	2
1 c.	skim milk	250 mL

Sift flour and salt together; set aside. Beat eggs and skim milk; add to flour. Beat until smooth and creamy. Pour into heated greased muffin tins, filling half full or less. Bake at 375° F (190° C) for 50 minutes, or until popovers are golden brown and sound hollow. DO NOT OPEN OVEN FOR FIRST 40 MINUTES.

Yield: 18 popovers
Exchange 1 popover: ½ bread
½ meat
Calories 1 popover: 44

Soya Crisps

1 c.	soya flour	250 mL
1 c.	chicken broth	250 mL
1 T.	liquid shortening	15 mL
1 t.	salt	5 mL

Blend soya flour and broth in saucepan until smooth. Bring gradually to a boil; remove from heat. Blend in liquid shortening and salt. Pour into large flat baking sheet to a depth of no more than ¼ in. (6 mm). Bake at 325° F (165° C) for 30 minutes. Cool slightly. Cut into 2¼-in. (6-cm) squares. Cut diagonally into triangles.

Yield: 80 chips
Exchange 10 chips: 1 lean meat
Calories 10 chips: 50

Cake Doughnuts

1 T.	granulated sugar	15 mL
4 T.	sugar replacement	60 mL
⅓ c.	buttermilk	80 mL
1	egg (well beaten)	1
1 c.	flour	250 mL
⅛ t.	baking soda	1 mL
1 t.	baking powder	5 mL
dash each	nutmeg, cinnamon, vanilla extract, salt	dash each
	oil for deep-fat frying	

Combine sugars, buttermilk, and egg; beat well. Add remaining ingredients, except oil. Beat just until blended. Heat oil to 375° F (190° C). Drop dough from doughnut dropper into hot fat. Fry until golden brown, turning often. Drain.

Yield: 12 doughnuts
Exchange 1 doughnut: 1 bread
1 fat
Calories 1 doughnut: 130

Scone Variations

Stir one of the following into flour mixture for Tea Scones:

Apple

8 chopped, dried apple halves

Exchange 1 scone: 1 bread
                   ¼ fruit

Calories 1 scone: 44

Apricot

8 chopped, dried apricot halves

Exchange 1 scone: 1 bread
                   ¼ fruit

Calories 1 scone: 44

Cranberry

¼ c. (60 mL) chopped cranberries

Exchange 1 scone: 1 bread

Calories 1 scone: 34

Dates

8 chopped dates

Exchange 1 scone: 1 bread
                   ½ fruit

Calories 1 scone: 54

Lemon

1 T. (15 mL) grated lemon peel

Exchange 1 scone: 1 bread

Calories 1 scone: 34

Orange

1½ T. (25 mL) grated orange peel

Exchange 1 scone: 1 bread

Calories 1 scone: 34

Peaches

8 chopped dried peach halves

Exchange 1 scone: 1 fruit
                   ½ bread

Calories 1 scone: 54

Raisin

4 T. (60 mL) raisins

Exchange 1 scone: 1 bread
                   ¼ fruit

Calories 1 scone: 44

Tea Scones

1 c.	flour	250 mL
1 t.	baking powder	5 mL
¼ t.	salt	2 mL
1 T.	sugar replacement	15 mL
¼ c.	margarine (cold)	60 mL
1	egg	1
¼ c.	evaporated (skim) milk	60 mL

Sift flour, baking powder, salt, and sugar replacement. Cut in cold margarine as for pie crust. Beat egg and evaporated milk together thoroughly; stir into flour mixture. Knead gently on lightly floured board. Divide dough in half; roll each half into a circle. Cut circles into quarters. Place on lightly greased cookie sheet. Brush tops with milk. Bake at 450° F (230° C) for 15 minutes, or until done.

Yield: 8 scones
Exchange 1 scone: 1 bread
Calories 1 scone: 34

Potato Dumplings

1 small	cooked potato	1 small
1	egg (beaten)	1
2 T.	flour	30 mL
	salt and pepper to taste	

With a fork, break up and mash the potato. Combine with the remaining ingredients. Beat untl light and fluffy. Drop by tablespoonfuls on top of boiling salted water or beef broth. Boil for 5 minutes, or until dumplings rise to surface. Good with Sauerbraten (p. 55).

Yield: 3 or 4 dumplings
Exchange: 1 bread
1 meat
Calories: 140

Baked Sweet Potato

¼ c.	sweet potato or yam (mashed)	60 mL
dash each	salt, pepper, nutmeg	dash each
1 T.	milk	15 mL

Combine all ingredients. Beat until smooth and creamy. Bake at 350° F (175° C) for 20 minutes.

Yield: 1 serving
Exchange: 1 bread
Calories: 75

Mountain Man Pancakes

1	egg	1
1¼ c.	buttermilk	310 mL
1 T.	molasses	15 mL
2 T.	margarine (melted)	30 mL
1 c.	flour	250 mL
1 t.	salt	5 mL
½ t.	baking soda	3 mL
2 t.	baking powder	10 mL
½ c.	yellow cornmeal	125 mL
	vegetable cooking spray	

Beat egg, buttermilk, molasses, and margarine together until well blended. Add remaining ingredients, except vegetable cooking spray. Stir just enough to blend. Cook in skillet coated with vegetable cooking spray.

Yield: 10 pancakes, 4 in. (9 cm) in diameter each
Exchange 1 pancake: 1 bread
1 fat
Calories 1 pancake: 95

Potato Pancake

1 medium	raw potato (grated)	1 medium
1	egg	1
2 T.	flour	30 mL
2 t.	salt	10 mL
2 t.	chives	10 mL
	vegetable cooking spray	

Place grated potato in ice water. Allow to stand for 30 minutes to an hour. Drain; pat potato dry. Place potato in bowl; add egg, flour, salt, and chives. Stir to blend. Divide mixture into 4 parts and spoon into large skillet coated with vegetable cooking spray. Brown on both sides.

Yield: 4 pancakes
Exchange 2 pancakes: 1 bread
½ medium-fat meat
Calories 2 pancakes: 80

Potato Puffs

½ c.	potatoes (cooked and mashed or whipped)	125 mL
1 c.	flour	250 mL
1½ t.	baking powder	8 mL
½ t.	salt	3 mL
1	egg (well beaten)	1
½ c.	milk	125 mL
	oil for deep-fat frying	

With a fork, break up and mash enough potatoes to fill a small cup. Combine with remaining ingredients, except oil. Beat well. Heat oil to 375° F (190° C). From tablespoon, drop a walnut-size piece of dough into hot fat. Remove when puff rises to the surface (about 2–3 minutes) and is golden brown. Repeat with remaining dough. Drain.

Yield: 24 puffs
Exchange 2 puffs: 1 bread
1½ fat
Calories 2 puffs: 160

Cornbread Stuffing

6 T.	butter	90 mL
1 large	onion (chopped)	1 large
1 c.	celery with tops (chopped)	250 mL
1 t.	thyme	5 mL
1 t.	sage	5 mL
1 T.	salt	15 mL
1 t.	pepper	5 mL
6 c.	cornbread crumbs	1.5 L

Melt butter in medium saucepan. Add onion, celery, thyme, sage, salt, and pepper. Sauté over low heat for 3 to 4 minutes. Remove from heat. Add cornbread crumbs; toss to mix. Add water to moisten to stuffing consistency.

Yield: 6 c. (1500 mL)
Exchange ½ c. (125 mL): 1 bread
1 fat
Calories ½ c. (125 mL): 125

Prune-Apple Stuffing

1 c.	prunes (soaked and chopped)	250 mL
1½ c.	apples (chopped)	375 mL
½ c.	raisins	125 mL
1 t.	cinnamon	5 mL
½ t.	nutmeg	3 mL

Combine fruit and spices; mix thoroughly. Allow to rest for 10 minutes before using.

Yield: 3 c. (750 mL)
Exchange ¼ c. (60 mL): 1 fruit
Calories ¼ c. (60 mL): 60

Herb-Seasoned Stuffing

1-lb. loaf	bread (2 to 3 days old)	500-g loaf
½ c.	butter or margarine	125 mL
1 t.	thyme	5 mL
1 t.	sage	5 mL
1 t.	rosemary	5 mL
1 t.	dried lemon rind	5 mL

Remove crust from bread; cut bread into cubes. Melt butter or margarine in large skillet. Add seasonings; stir to mix. Add bread cubes. Toss or stir lightly to coat bread cubes. Pour onto baking sheet. Allow to dry by air or dry in very slow oven. These dried bread cubes are good as croutons; add salt and water to moisten when ready to use as stuffing.

Yield: 8 c. (2 L)
Exchange ½ c. (125 mL): 1 bread
1 fat
Calories ½ c. (125 mL): 75

Baked Rice

1 cube	beef bouillon	1 cube
1 c.	hot water	250 mL
¼ c.	rice	60 mL
1	green onion (chopped)	1
2 T.	celery (chopped)	30 mL
3 T.	dry bread crumbs	45 mL

Dissolve bouillon in hot water. Add rice, green onion, and celery; cover. Cook for 5 minutes. Add bread crumbs. Pour into small baking dish. Bake at 350° F (175° C) for 25 to 30 minutes, or until top is lightly crusted.

Yield: 1 serving
Exchange: 1½ bread
Calories: 115

Rice Pilaf

½ c.	rice	125 mL
1 t.	butter	5 mL
½ t.	salt	3 mL
1 T.	lemon juice	15 mL
1 c.	boiling water	250 mL

Sauté rice in butter over low heat in large saucepan. Add remaining ingredients. Bring to a boil. Reduce heat; cover. Simmer until water is absorbed. Fluff with fork before serving.

Yield: 1 c. (250 mL)
Exchange: 2 bread
1 fat
Calories: 150

Corn Pudding

16-oz. can	corn	500-g can
1	egg (beaten)	1
1 t.	pimiento (chopped)	5 mL
1 t.	green pepper	5 mL
1 t.	margarine (melted)	5 mL
1 t.	sugar replacement	5 mL
¾ c.	milk	180 mL
	salt and pepper to taste	
	vegetable cooking spray	

Combine all ingredients, except vegetable cooking spray. Pour into baking dish coated with vegetable cooking spray. Bake at 325° F (165° C) for 35 to 40 minutes, or until firm.

Yield: 6 servings
Exchange 1 serving: 1 bread
1 fat
Calories 1 serving: 55

VEGETABLES

ABC's of Vegetables

1 c.	asparagus pieces	250 mL
1 c.	broccoli flowerets	250 mL
1 c.	carrot slices	250 mL
1 c.	spinach (chopped)	250 mL
	vegetable cooking spray	
11-oz. can	condensed cream of mushroom soup	300-g can
2 T.	onions (finely chopped)	30 mL
1 t.	thyme	5 mL
½ c.	water	125 mL
	salt and pepper to taste	

Layer asparagus, broccoli, carrots, and spinach in a baking dish coated with vegetable cooking spray. Blend remaining ingredients. Pour over vegetables. Cover. Bake at 350° F (175° C) for 30 to 40 minutes, or until vegetables are tender.

Yield: 8 servings
Exchange 1 serving: 1 vegetable
½ bread
½ fat
Calories 1 serving: 42

Baked Eggplant

1 slice	eggplant	1 slice
1 slice	onion	1 slice
1 oz.	sharp Cheddar cheese (shredded)	30 g
2 T.	condensed tomato soup	30 mL
1 t.	dry bread crumbs	5 mL
¼ t.	thyme	1 mL
¼ t.	salt	1 mL
dash	pepper	dash

Cook eggplant and onion in small amount of water until tender. Drain; reserve liquid. Place eggplant and onion in small baking dish. Top with cheese. Blend condensed soup, 1 T. (15 mL) of the eggplant liquid, bread crumbs, thyme, salt, and pepper. Pour over eggplant; cover. Bake at 350° F (175° C) for 30 minutes.

Microwave: Uncover. Cook on High for 5 minutes. Turn after 2 minutes.

Yield: 1 serving
Exchange: 1 high-fat meat
1 vegetable
Calories: 161

Cheese Tomato

1	tomato (thickly sliced)	1
	vegetable cooking spray	
dash each	celery salt, garlic salt, pepper	dash each
1 oz.	American cheese (grated)	30 g

Place tomato slices on broiler pan coated with vegetable cooking spray. Sprinkle with seasonings. Top with cheese. Broil 5 to 6 in. (15 cm) from heat until cheese is melted.

Yield: 1 serving
Exchange: 1 vegetable
1 high-fat meat
Calories: 140

Okra and Tomatoes

2 c.	okra	500 mL
¼ c.	vinegar	60 mL
2 c.	tomatoes (cut into eighths)	500 mL
1 c.	onions (coarsely chopped)	250 mL
½ c.	green pepper (coarsely chopped)	125 mL
sprig	parsley (chopped)	sprig
1 T.	mint (chopped)	15 mL
1 t.	garlic powder	5 mL
	salt and pepper to taste	
	vegetable cooking spray	

Soak okra in vinegar for 5 minutes. Drain. Pat okra slightly dry. Combine all ingredients (except vinegar) in baking dish coated with vegetable cooking spray. Cover. Bake at 350° F (175° C) for 45 minutes.

Yield: 5 servings
Exchange 1 serving: 1 vegetable
Calories 1 serving: 31

Kohlrabi

2 c.	kohlrabi (cut into strips)	500 mL
2 t.	butter	10 mL
2 T.	fresh parsley (chopped)	30 mL
	salt and pepper to taste	

Cook kohlrabi in boiling salted water until soft; drain. Melt butter or margarine in saucepan. Add parsley; sauté over low heat for 2 minutes. Add kohlrabi. Toss to coat. Add salt and pepper.

Yield: 4 servings
Exchange 1 serving: 1 vegetable
½ fat
Calories 1 serving: 36

Italian Asparagus

½ lb.	asparagus spears (cooked or canned)	250 g
	vegetable cooking spray	
¼ c.	Tomato Sauce (p. 128)	60 mL
¼ c.	water	60 mL
½ t.	oregano	3 mL
¼ t.	garlic powder	1 mL
	salt and pepper to taste	
¼ c.	Swiss cheese (grated)	60 mL

Lay asparagus spears in shallow baking dish coated with vegetable cooking spray. Blend Tomato Sauce, water, oregano, garlic powder, salt, and pepper. Spread evenly over spears. Top with grated cheese. Bake at 350° F (175° C) for 20–25 minutes.

Microwave: Cook on High for 5–6 minutes.

Yield: 4 servings
Exchange 1 serving: ½ vegetable
½ medium-fat meat
Calories 1 serving: 58

Cauliflower au Gratin

2 c.	cauliflowerets	500 mL
1 t.	salt	5 mL
1 t.	butter	5 mL
1 t.	flour	5 mL
1 c.	milk (cold)	250 mL
¼ c.	American cheese (diced)	60 mL
	vegetable cooking spray	
	salt and pepper to taste	

Place cauliflowerets in large kettle. Fill with enough water to cover. Add salt. Bring to a boil; cook 5 minutes. Drain;

rinse with cold water. Melt butter or margarine in saucepan. Blend flour with cold milk. Add to melted butter. Cook over low heat, stirring constantly, until slightly thickened. Add cheese; cook until cheese is completely blended. Place cauliflower in baking dish coated with vegetable cooking spray; add salt and pepper. Cover with cheese topping. Bake at 350° F (175° C) for 20 minutes.

Yield: 4 servings
Exchange 1 serving: 1 vegetable
                                    ½ medium-fat meat
Calories 1 serving: 119

Brussels Sprouts and Mushrooms au Gratin

1 T.	butter	15 mL
2 c.	Brussels sprouts	500 mL
1 c.	mushroom pieces	250 mL
	salt and pepper to taste	
2 oz.	Swiss cheese (grated)	60 g

Melt butter in skillet. Lightly sauté Brussels sprouts and mushrooms. Add salt and pepper. Remove from heat and pour into baking dish. Cover with cheese. Bake at 350° F (175° C) for 20 to 25 minutes.

Microwave: Cook on Medium for 10 minutes. Turn once.

Yield: 4 servings
Exchange 1 serving: 1 high-fat meat
                                    ½ vegetable
Calories 1 serving: 65

Baked Vegetable Medley

1 c.	2-in. (5-cm) cubes eggplant	250 mL
1 c.	2-in. (5-cm) slices okra	250 mL
1 c.	bean sprouts	250 mL
½ c.	small mushrooms	125 mL
1	onion (cut into eighths)	1
	vegetable cooking spray	
11-oz. can	condensed cream of celery soup	300-g can
¼ c.	water	60 mL
	salt and pepper to taste	
1 slice	bread (finely crumbled)	1 slice

Combine all vegetables in baking dish coated with vegetable cooking spray. Blend condensed soup and water; add salt and pepper. Pour over vegetables. Top with bread crumbs. Cook at 325° F (165° C) for 25 to 30 minutes, or until hot, and crumbs are golden brown.

Yield: 8 servings
Exchange 1 serving: 1 vegetable
½ bread
Calories 1 serving: 49

Shredded Cabbage

1 head	cabbage (coarsely shredded)	1 head
2 t.	butter	10 mL
½ t.	nutmeg	2 mL
	salt and pepper to taste	

Cook cabbage in a small amount of boiling salted water until tender; drain. Press out excess moisture or pat dry. Melt butter in skillet. Add nutmeg; stir to blend. Add cabbage; toss to coat. Add salt and pepper.

Yield: 4 servings
Exchange 1 serving: ½ vegetable
½ fat
Calories 1 serving: 32

Irish Vegetables

1	bay leaf	1
1 c.	water	250 mL
2 T.	wine vinegar	30 mL
½ c.	corn	125 mL
½ c.	celery (sliced)	125 mL
½ c.	broccoli flowerets	125 mL
½ c.	carrot (sliced)	125 mL
½ c.	cauliflowerets	125 mL
¼ c.	pimiento (chopped)	60 mL
	salt and pepper to taste	

Combine bay leaf, water, and wine vinegar in medium saucepan. Bring to a boil; add vegetables. Simmer until vegetables are tender. Drain; remove bay leaf. Add salt and pepper.

Yield: 5 servings
Exchange 1 serving: 1 bread
Calories 1 serving: 51

Spiced Bean Sprouts

2 c.	bean sprouts	500 mL
½ t.	caraway seeds	2 mL
½ t.	basil	2 mL
2 t.	butter	10 mL
	salt and pepper to taste	

Combine bean sprouts, caraway seeds, and basil in saucepan with small amount of water. Cook until hot and tender; drain. Place in serving dish; top with butter, salt, and pepper. Toss to coat.

Yield: 4 servings
Exchange 1 serving: ¼ vegetable
                       ½ fat
Calories 1 serving: 25

German Green Beans

2 c.	green beans	500 mL
1 slice	bacon	1 slice
¼ c.	onion (chopped)	60 mL
1 t.	flour	5 mL
¼ c.	vinegar	60 mL
½ c.	water	125 mL
2 T.	sugar replacement	30 mL

Cook green beans in boiling salted water until tender; drain. Cut bacon into ½-in. (12-mm) pieces. Place in skillet; add onion. Sauté until bacon is crisp and onion is tender; drain. Blend flour, vinegar, water, and sugar replacement in screwtop jar. Pour over bacon and onion. Cook over low heat to thicken slightly. Add green beans.

Yield: 4 servings
Exchange 1 serving: ½ vegetable
                       ¼ bread
                       ½ fat
Calories 1 serving: 52

Pizza Beans

2 c.	green beans	500 mL
1 T.	lemon juice	15 mL
¼ t.	oregano	1 mL
1 t.	pimiento (chopped)	5 mL
dash each	garlic powder, salt	dash each

Cook green beans in boiling salted water until tender; drain. Combine lemon juice, oregano, pimiento, garlic powder, and salt. Pour over beans; toss.

Yield: 5 servings
Exchange 1 serving: 1 vegetable
Calories 1 serving: 32

Whipped Summer Squash

3 c.	summer squash	750 mL
¼ c.	evaporated milk	60 mL
2 t.	butter	10 mL
	salt and pepper to taste	

Peel and cut squash into small pieces. Place in saucepan with small amount of water. Bring to a boil; reduce heat and simmer until squash is crisp-tender. Drain. Beat squash with rotary beater; add evaporated milk and butter. Beat until light and fluffy. Add salt and pepper.

Yield: 4 servings
Exchange 1 serving: 1 vegetable
1 fat
Calories 1 serving: 68

Spiced Beets

½ c.	wine vinegar	125 mL
¼ c.	water	60 mL
1	bay leaf	1
1	whole clove	1
1 t.	black pepper	5 mL
3 T.	sugar replacement	45 mL
2 c.	beets (sliced)	500 mL

Combine all ingredients except beets. Bring to a boil. Add beets; simmer for 10 minutes, or until tender.

Microwave: Combine all ingredients, except beets. Cook on High for 2 minutes. Add beets. Cook on Medium for 2 minutes

Yield: 4 servings
Exchange 1 serving: 1 bread
Calories 1 serving: 36

Indian Squash

2 c	acorn squash (cubed)	500 mL
2 t.	margarine	10 mL
1 t.	orange rind	5 mL
¼ c.	orange juice	60 mL
2 T.	sugar replacement	30 mL

Cook squash in small amount of boiling water until crisp-tender; drain. Melt margarine in saucepan. Add orange rind, juice, and sugar replacement. Cook over low heat until sugar is dissolved. Add squash; cover. Continue cooking until squash is tender.

Yield: 4 servings
Exchange 1 serving: 1 bread
½ fat
Calories 1 serving: 60

Beans Orientale

1½ c.	French-cut green beans (cooked)	375 mL
2 T.	almonds (blanched and slivered)	30 mL
½ c.	mushroom pieces	125 mL
2 t.	butter	10 mL
	salt and pepper to taste	

Heat green beans; drain. Sauté almonds and mushrooms in butter. Add green beans. Add salt and pepper.

Microwave: Melt butter in bowl. Add almonds and mushrooms. Cover. Cook on High for 30 seconds. Add green beans. Cook on Medium for 2 to 3 minutes.

Yield: 4 servings
Exchange 1 serving: ½ vegetable
½ fat
Calories 1 serving: 45

Vegetable Casserole

1 c.	peas	250 mL
1 c.	green beans	250 mL
1 c.	carrots (sliced)	250 mL
1 c.	mushrooms	250 mL
1	egg	1
1 t.	margarine (melted)	5 mL
½ c.	milk	125 mL
	salt and pepper to taste	
	vegetable cooking spray	

Cook vegetables in small amount of boiling salted water until crisp-tender; drain. Chop vegetables fine. Whip egg until lemon colored; add margarine and milk. Blend well. Add chopped vegetables, salt, and pepper. Pour into baking dish coated with vegetable cooking spray. Cover. Bake at 350° F (175° C) for 45 minutes, or until set.

Yield: 8 servings
Exchange 1 serving: 1 vegetable
Calories 1 serving: 36

Pea Pod—Carrot Sauté

1 c.	pea pods	250 mL
1 c.	carrots (sliced)	250 mL
1 t.	salt	5 mL
2 t.	margarine	10 mL
1 T.	Worcestershire sauce	15 mL

Combine pea pods and carrots in saucepan. Cover with water; add salt. Cook until tender; drain. Melt margarine in saucepan. Add Worcestershire sauce; stir to blend. Add pea pods and carrots. Toss to coat.

Yield: 4 servings
Exchange 1 serving: ½ bread
  ½ fat
Calories 1 serving: 50

Circus Carrots

2 c.	carrots (finger- or julienne-cut)	500 mL
2 t.	butter	10 mL
2 T.	lemon juice	30 mL
2 t.	parsley flakes	10 mL

Cook carrots in boiling salted water until tender; keep warm. Melt butter; add lemon juice and parsley flakes. Add warm carrots; toss to coat.

Microwave: Cook carrots in small amount of water on High for 2 minutes. Drain. Add remaining ingredients. Cover. Cook on High for 2 minutes. Toss to mix.

Yield: 4 servings
Exchange 1 serving: ¼ fat
1 bread
Calories 1 serving: 59

Candied Carrot Squares

4	carrots	4
1 t.	salt	5 mL
2 T.	brown sugar replacement	30 mL
2 t.	butter	10 mL
½ c.	lo-cal cream (or any white) soda	125 mL

Cut carrots into lengths to make squares. Place carrots in saucepan and cover with water; add salt. Cook until crisp-tender; drain. Place in baking dish. Sprinkle carrots with brown sugar replacement; dot with butter; add white soda. Bake at 350° F (175° C) for 30 minutes. Turn carrots gently two or three times during baking.

Yield: 4 servings
Exchange 1 serving: 1 bread
½ fat
Calories 1 serving: 47

Spinach with Onion

2 lb.	fresh spinach	1 kg
2 t.	margarine	10 mL
½ c.	onion (sliced)	125 mL
dash each	nutmeg, thyme, salt, pepper	dash each

Rinse spinach thoroughly; place in top of double boiler and heat until wilted. Drain and chop coarsely. Melt margarine in skillet; add onion. Sauté over high heat until onion is brown on the edges. Add seasonings. Stir to blend. Add spinach and toss to blend.

Yield: 4 servings
Exchange 1 serving: ½ vegetable
½ fat
Calories 1 serving: 37

Zucchini Florentine

4 small	zucchini	4 small
2 t.	margarine	10 mL
1 c.	fresh spinach (chopped)	250 mL
1 c.	skim milk	250 mL
3	eggs (slightly beaten)	3
1 t.	salt	5 mL
¼ t.	pepper	1 mL
¼ t.	thyme	1 mL
¼ t.	paprika	1 mL

Cut zucchini into thin slices. Melt margarine in baking dish; add zucchini. Bake at 400° F (200° C) for 15 minutes. Add spinach. Blend skim milk, eggs, salt, pepper, and thyme. Pour over vegetables. Sprinkle with paprika. Bake at 350° F (175° C) for 40 minutes, or until set.

Yield: 6 servings
Exchange 1 serving: 1 vegetable
½ high-fat meat
Calories 1 serving: 82

Zucchini Wedges

4 small	zucchini	4 small
2 t.	margarine	10 mL
2 t.	onion (grated)	10 mL
1 cube	beef bouillon	1 cube
2 T.	boiling water	30 mL

Cut zucchini in half lengthwise. Melt margarine in skillet. Add onion and bouillon cube. Press bouillon cube against bottom of skillet to crush. Stir to blend. Place zucchini cut side down in skillet. Sauté until golden brown; turn. Add boiling water; cover. Cook over low heat for 10 minutes, or until tender.

Yield: 4 servings
Exchange 1 serving: ½ vegetable
½ fat
Calories 1 serving: 37

SALADS

Perfect Salad

½ env.	unflavored gelatin	½ env.
¼ c.	cold water	60 mL
1 T.	sugar replacement	15 mL
½ t.	salt	2 mL
¾ c.	hot water	180 mL
1 T.	lemon juice	15 mL
2	cucumbers (grated)	2
¼ c	carrot (grated)	60 mL
¼ c	onion (chopped)	60 mL
3 oz.	cream cheese	90 g
2 T.	lo-cal mayonnaise	30 mL

Dissolve gelatin in cold water. Add gelatin mixture, sugar replacement, and salt to hot water; stir until dissolved. Add lemon juice, cucumbers, carrot, and onion. Beat cream cheese with mayonnaise until smooth. Blend into vegetable mixture. Pour into mold and chill.

Yield: 8 servings
Exchange 1 serving: ½ vegetable
1 fat
Calories 1 serving: 73

Mushroom Salad

½ head	iceberg lettuce	½ head
½ head	Boston lettuce	½ head
1	cucumber	1
½ lb.	green beans	250 g
½ lb.	mushrooms	250 g
¼ c.	lo-cal French dressing	60 mL

Rinse lettuce. Break into large pieces. Peel and slice cucumber into ¼-in. (6-mm) slices. Rinse green beans; cut beans into 1-in. (2.5-cm) pieces. Place greens, cucumber, and beans into plastic bag or tightly covered container. Store in refrigerator 4 to 6 hours or overnight to crisp. Trim mushroom stems to ¼-in. (6-mm) of cap. (Peel mushrooms if discolored.) Cut mushrooms in thin slices. Just before serving, carefully pat greens, cucumber, and beans dry on towel. Place in wooden bowl; cover with French dressing. Toss to lightly coat all ingredients with dressing. Top with mushrooms.

Yield: 8 servings
Exchange 1 serving: 1 vegetable
Calories 1 serving: 60

Chinese Salad

1 head	Bibb lettuce	1 head
1 head	Boston lettuce	1 head
2 stalks	Chinese cabbage	2 stalks
8-oz. can	water chestnuts	225-g can
8-oz. can	bamboo shoots	225-g can
1 c.	bean sprouts	250 mL
½ c.	Soy French Dressing (p. 130)	125 mL

Rinse lettuce and cabbage leaves. Break into bite-size pieces. Place in plastic bag or tightly covered container. Store in refrigerator 4 to 6 hours or overnight to crisp. Drain water chestnuts, bamboo shoots, and bean sprouts. Rinse with cold water. Drain thoroughly. Thinly slice the water chestnuts. Carefully pat greens dry with towel. Place in wooden bowl. Top with water chestnuts, bamboo shoots, and bean sprouts. Cover with Soy French Dressing. Toss lightly until all ingredients are coated.

Yield: 12 servings
Exchange 1 serving: ½ vegetable
Calories 1 serving: 40

Dandelion Salad

1 c.	young dandelion greens	250 mL
1 head	iceberg lettuce	1 head
2 T.	lo-cal Italian dressing	30 mL
2	tomatoes	2
1 small	cucumber	1 small
2 T.	lo-cal bleu cheese dressing	30 mL
1 T.	skim milk	15 mL

Rinse greens and lettuce. Pat dry with towel. Break into large pieces. Place in large plastic bag. Sprinkle with Italian dressing. Close tightly and store in refrigerator to crisp. Shake occasionally. Peel tomatoes and remove seeds; slice tomato flesh into strips. Peel cucumber; slice into ⅛-in. (3-mm) slices. Place greens, lettuce, tomatoes, and cucumber in wooden bowl. Blend bleu cheese dressing with skim milk. Cover salad with dressing. Toss to coat all ingredients.

Yield: 6 servings
Exchange 1 serving: Negligible
Calories 1 serving: Negligible
Added Touch: Top each serving with a few Garlic Croutons (p. 15). Add exchange and calories for croutons.

Jean's Vegetable Salad

1 c.	asparagus, cut into 2-in. (5-cm) pieces	250 mL
1 c.	broccoli flowerets	250 mL
1 c.	cauliflowerets	250 mL
½ c.	celery (sliced)	125 mL
½ c.	cucumber (scored and sliced)	125 mL
1 c.	fresh mushrooms (sliced)	250 mL
1 c.	green pepper (sliced)	250 mL
½ c.	radishes (sliced)	125 mL
10	pitted black olives (sliced)	10
½ c.	lo-cal Italian dressing	125 mL

Combine all vegetables in large bowl. Cover with Italian dressing. Marinate overnight. Toss frequently.

Yield: 7 servings
Exchange 1 serving: 1 vegetable
Calories 1 serving: 45

Radish Salad

1 t.	salt	5 mL
1 t.	garlic powder	5 mL
1 t.	Dijon mustard	5 mL
1 T.	wine vinegar	15 mL
2 T.	liquid shortening	30 mL
2 t.	lemon juice	10 mL
1	watercress (small bunch)	1
½ head	iceberg lettuce	½ head
1 bunch	red radishes	1 bunch

Combine salt, garlic powder, Dijon mustard, vinegar, liquid shortening, and lemon juice in screwtop jar. Shake to blend. Coarsely chop watercress, lettuce and radishes; place in salad bowl. Add dressing; toss to blend.

Yield: 6 servings
Exchange 1 serving: 1 fat
Calories 1 serving: 60

Maude's Green Salad

½ head	iceberg lettuce	½ head
½ head	Boston lettuce	½ head
½ head	chicory	½ head
½ lb.	spinach	250 g
½ head	romaine lettuce	½ head
5 T.	lo-cal Italian dressing	75 mL
1 T.	Parmesan cheese	15 mL

Rinse and crisp the salad greens. Break iceberg lettuce into bite-size pieces. Carefully pat iceberg dry on towel. Place in large plastic bag. Add 1 T. (15 mL) Italian dressing. Shake lightly until all leaves are covered. Place in strip on medium platter or plate. Repeat with each green. Sprinkle lightly with Parmesan cheese.

Yield: 10 servings
Exchange: Negligible
Calories: Negligible

German Potato Salad

6 slices	bacon (crispy fried)	6 slices
1½ c.	cold water	375 mL
3 T.	flour	45 mL
1 medium	onion (chopped)	1 medium
3 T.	sugar replacement	45 mL
¼ c.	vinegar	60 mL
6 medium	boiled potatoes (sliced)	6 medium

Remove excess grease from bacon with paper towel. Break bacon into small pieces. Blend cold water and flour. Pour into saucepan. Add onion, sugar replacement, and vinegar. Heat, stirring, until thickened. Add bacon and potatoes while still warm from boiling and frying.

Yield: 8 servings
Exchange 1 serving: 1 bread
1 fat
Calories 1 serving: 113

Swiss Salad

1 small head	iceberg lettuce	1 small head
1 head	romaine lettuce	1 head
¼ lb.	fresh spinach	125 g
1 large	cucumber	1 large
1	green pepper	1
1 c.	cherry tomatoes	250 mL
½ c.	lo-cal French dressing	125 mL

Rinse and wash greens. Drain thoroughly. Break into large pieces; place in plastic bag or tightly covered container. Store in refrigerator 4 to 6 hours or overnight to crisp. Score cucumber with tines of fork. Cut into ⅛-in. (3-mm) slices. Cut green pepper into thin rings. Cut cherry tomatoes in half. Just before serving, carefully pat greens dry on towel. Place greens in large wooden bowl; cover with French dressing. Toss greens lightly, coating all leaves with dressing. Top with cucumber, green pepper, and cherry tomatoes. Serve immediately.

Yield: 16 servings
Exchange 1 serving: ½ vegetable
Calories 1 serving: 32

Marinated Cucumbers

2 to 3	cucumbers (large)	2 to 3
1 t.	salt	5 mL
1 t.	sugar replacement	5 mL
¼ c.	vinegar	60 mL
⅛ t.	pepper	1 mL

Score cucumbers with tines of fork. Cut into very thin slices. Sprinkle with salt. Chill 2 hours; drain well. Sprinkle with sugar replacement; add vinegar and pepper. Marinate 30 minutes or more before serving.

Yield: 6 to 8 servings
Exchange: Negligible
Calories: Negligible

Asparagus Salad

¼ lb.	spinach	125 g
1 head	romaine lettuce	1 head
10 spears	raw asparagus	10 spears
½ head	red cabbage	½ head
½ c.	celery (sliced)	125 mL
½	cucumber (peeled and sliced)	½
½ c.	Lemon French Dressing (p. 130)	125 mL

Rinse greens. Break into bite-size pieces. Place in plastic bag or tightly covered container. Store in refrigerator 4 to 6 hours or overnight to crisp. Wash asparagus spears and cut into 2-in. (5-cm) pieces. Shred cabbage as for coleslaw; remove all hard pieces. Just before serving, carefully pat greens dry on towel. Place all ingredients in wooden bowl. Toss lightly to coat all ingredients with Lemon French Dressing.

Yield: 12 servings
Exchange 1 serving: ½ vegetable
Calories 1 serving 42

Hot Green Pepper Salad

4	green peppers	4
1 T.	butter	15 mL
1 t.	oregano	5 mL
½ t.	thyme	2 mL
	salt and pepper to taste	
½ c.	mushroom pieces	125 mL

Rinse green peppers. Cut them into quarters. Melt butter in skillet. Add seasonings, green peppers, and mushrooms. Cook over low heat for 10 minutes. Serve immediately.

Yield: 4 servings
Exchange 1 serving: 1 vegetable
1 fat
Calories 1 serving: 60

Shrimp and Green Bean Salad

2 c.	green beans	500 mL
2 c.	shrimp	500 mL
½ c.	mushrooms (thinly sliced)	125 mL
¼ c.	Bay Salad Dressing (p. 132)	60 mL
	lettuce leaves	

Rinse and snap green beans. Cook in small amount of boiling salted water until crisp-tender. Drain and cool immediately in ice water; chill. Clean and devein shrimp, or use canned shrimp. Rinse thoroughly under cold water; chill. Combine green beans, shrimp, and mushrooms in bowl. Sprinkle with Bay Salad Dressing. Toss to coat. Chill thoroughly before serving. Serve on lettuce leaves.

Yield: 4 servings
Exchange 1 serving: 1 lean meat
½ vegetable
Calories 1 serving: 62

Salmon Salad Plate

1 oz.	cold salmon (cooked)	30 g
½ small	tomato	½ small
¼ c.	carrot sticks	60 mL
¼	green pepper (sliced)	¼
¼ c.	eggplant sticks	60 mL
1	egg (hard cooked)	1
1 T.	cottage cheese	15 mL
	salt and pepper to taste	
	lettuce leaf	

Chill salmon. Peel tomato and remove seeds; slice tomato flesh into strips. Cook carrot, green pepper, eggplant, and tomato in boiling salted water until crisp-tender. (Remember, the carrots sticks may take more time to cook than the other vegetables.) Drain and chill. Cut egg in half length-wise. Mash egg yolk with cottage cheese, salt, and pepper; stuff egg white halves. Arrange cooked salmon, vegetables, and stuffed eggs on crisp lettuce leaf.

Yield: 1 serving
Exchange: 2⅓ lean meat
              1 vegetable
Calories: 193

Waldorf Salad

1 c.	celery (sliced)	250 mL
1 c.	seedless green grapes (halved)	250 mL
1 c.	apple (diced)	250 mL
4	dates (pitted and thinly sliced)	4
½ c.	walnuts (chopped)	125 mL
¼ c.	mayonnaise	60 mL
2 T.	dry white wine	30 mL
	lettuce leaves	

Place celery, grapes, apple, dates, and walnuts into bowl. Blend mayonnaise with wine; pour into bowl. Stir to blend with celery, fruit and walnuts. Use slotted serving spoon to serve, shaking spoon slightly to remove excess dressing. Serve on crisp lettuce leaves.

Yield: 7 servings
Exchange 1 serving: 2 fruit
                        ¼ vegetable
                        1 fat
Calories 1 serving: 105

Herring Salad Plate

1 oz.	salted herring	30 g
½ small	onion (thinly sliced)	½ small
¼ c.	beets (sliced)	60 mL
	Italian or French dressing	
	lettuce leaf	

Soak herring overnight in water. Remove skin and bones. Cut into 1-in. (2.5-cm) pieces. Place herring, onion, and beets in glass bowl. Cover with dressing. Marinate 4 to 5 hours or overnight. Drain. (Keep liquid; it makes a very good salad dressing.) Arrange herring, onion, and beets on crisp lettuce leaf.

Yield: 2 servings
Exchange 1 serving: ½ lean meat
1 bread
Calories 1 serving: 50

Lime Avocado Salad

1 pkg. (⅝ oz.)	lo-cal lime gelatin (both envelopes)	1 pkg. (20 g)
1½ c.	boiling water	375 mL
3 oz.	cream cheese	90 g
½ c.	lo-cal whipped topping (prepared)	125 mL
½ c.	avocado (cubed)	125 mL
½ c.	unsweetened fruit cocktail	125 mL
	vegetable cooking spray	
	shredded lettuce	

Dissolve gelatin in boiling water. Cool to consistency of beaten egg whites. Beat cream cheese; blend into gelatin mixture. Fold prepared whipped topping into gelatin mixture. Chill until quite firm. Fold in avocado and fruit cocktail. Pour into 1-qt. (1-L) ring mold coated with vegetable cooking spray. Chill until set. Serve on bed of shredded lettuce.

Yield: 8 servings
Exchange 1 serving: ½ vegetable
½ lean meat
1 fat
Calories 1 serving: 78

Cantaloupe Bowl

4	strawberries	4
4	fresh pineapple cubes	4
1 t.	sugar replacement	5 mL
¼	6-in. (15-cm) cantaloupe	¼

Sprinkle strawberries and pineapple with sugar replacement. Fill hollow of cantaloupe with fruit mixture.

Yield: 1 serving
Exchange: 2 fruit
Calories: 90

Grapefruit Salad

¼ c.	cranberries	60 mL
1½ c	grapefruit sections	375 mL
1	apple (sliced)	1
2 T.	raisins	30 mL
½ c.	orange juice	125 mL
	lettuce leaves	

Prick cranberries with sharp fork. Combine with remaining ingredients, except lettuce. Marinate 4 to 6 hours or overnight, drain. Serve on crisp lettuce leaves.

Yield: 5 servings
Exchange 1 serving: 1 fruit
Calories 1 serving: 40

Cranberry Salad

1 pkg. (⅝ oz.)	lo-cal lemon gelatin	1 pkg. (20 g)
1 T.	sugar replacement	15 mL
1½ c.	boiling water	375 mL
1	orange	1
½ c.	cranberries	125 mL
½ c.	celery (chopped)	125 mL
½ c.	apple (chopped)	125 mL

Dissolve gelatin and sugar replacement in boiling water. Cool to consistency of beaten egg whites. Grind orange (with peel) and cranberries; combine with celery and apple. Fold into gelatin mixture. Pour into mold or serving bowl. Chill until firm.

Yield: 8 servings
Exchange 1 serving: 1 fruit
Calories 1 serving: 24

Queen's Layered Gelatin

1 pkg. (⅝ oz.)	lo-cal strawberry gelatin	1 pkg. (20 g)
	vegetable cooking spray	
1 pkg. (⅝ oz.)	lo-cal lemon gelatin	1 pkg. (20 g)
3 oz.	cream cheese	90 g
1 c.	lo-cal whipped topping (prepared)	250 mL
1 pkg. (⅝ oz.)	lo-cal orange gelatin	1 pkg. (20 g)
½ c.	unsweetened crushed pineapple (drained)	125 mL
½ c.	carrot (grated)	125 mL
	shredded lettuce	

Prepare strawberry gelatin as directed on package. Pour into 2-qt. (2-L) mold coated with vegetable cooking spray. Chill until firm. Prepare lemon gelatin as directed on package. Set until consistency of beaten egg whites. Whip cream cheese until light and fluffy. Fold into prepared whipped topping.

Fold cream cheese topping into lemon gelatin. Pour over strawberry gelatin in mold. Chill until firm. Prepare orange gelatin as directed on package. Set until consistency of beaten egg whites. Fold in pineapple and carrot. Pour over lemon gelatin in mold. Chill until firm. Serve on bed of shredded lettuce.

Yield: 8 servings
Exchange 1 serving: ½ vegetable
1 fat
Calories 1 serving: 57

Blueberry Salad

1½ c.	fresh or frozen blueberries	375 mL
2 t.	sugar replacement	10 mL
1 env.	unflavored gelatin	1 env.
2 t.	lemon juice	10 mL
1 c.	unsweetened crushed pineapple (drained)	250 mL
1 c.	lo-cal whipped topping (prepared)	250 mL

Place blueberries in saucepan. Sprinkle with sugar replacement. Allow to rest 30 minutes at room temperature; drain. Add enough boiling water to make 2 c. (500 mL). Sprinkle unflavored gelatin over surface. Stir to dissolve. Cook over low heat for 2 to 3 minutes. Allow to rest until cool. Add lemon juice. Remove ⅓ c. (90 mL) from blueberry mixture. Chill until set; reserve. Fold pineapple into remaining gelatin; chill until firm. Whip reserved gelatin until frothy. Fold in prepared whipped topping. Spread over blueberry gelatin. Chill until set.

Yield: 4 servings
Exchange 1 serving: ½ fruit
Calories 1 serving: 24

Cabbage-Pineapple Salad

3 c.	cabbage (shredded)	750 mL
1 lb. can	unsweetened pineapple (diced)	500-g can
2 T.	sugar replacement	30 mL
dash	salt	dash
½ c.	lo-cal whipped topping (prepared)	125 mL

Combine cabbage and pineapple with juice, sugar replacement and salt. Stir to dissolve sugar. Allow to rest at room temperature for 1½ to 2 hours. Drain thoroughly. Fold topping into cabbage mixture.

Yield: 4 servings
Exchange 1 serving: ½ fruit
Calories 1 serving: 28

NOTE: Lo-cal whipped topping can be made by mixing non-dairy whipped topping with water.

Fruit Bowl

¼ c.	cantaloupe balls	60 mL
⅛ c.	honeydew balls	30 mL
½ c.	watermelon balls	125 mL
¼ c.	fresh, unsweetened pineapple chunks	60 mL
	salt	
	lo-cal French dressing	
	lettuce	

Sprinkle each fruit with salt and French dressing. Combine all ingredients, except lettuce. Refrigerate 1 to 2 hours. Serve on small bed of lettuce.

Yield: 1 serving
Exchange: 1 fruit
Calories: 40

Fruit Salad

16-oz. can	unsweetened apricot halves	500-g can
16-oz. can	unsweetened pineapple chunks	500-g can
2 t.	lemon juice	10 mL
1 t.	cornstarch	5 mL
2 t.	sugar replacement	10 mL
1 t.	margarine	5 mL
1	apple (chopped)	1
1	banana (sliced)	1
	lo-cal whipped topping	

Drain juice from apricots and pineapple into saucepan; add lemon juice and cornstarch. Cook over low heat to thicken. Remove from heat; add sugar replacement and margarine. Stir to blend; cool slightly. Combine all fruit in bowl. Pour sauce over fruit.

Yield: 6 servings
Exchange 1 serving: 1 fruit
Calories 1 serving: 53
Added Touch: Top each serving with a dab of whipped topping.

SAUCES AND
SALAD DRESSINGS

Tomato Sauce

firm red tomatoes (or canned
tomatoes without seasonings)

Quarter the tomatoes. Place in large kettle. Push down with
hands or back of spoon to render some juice. Bake at 325° F
(165° C) until soft pulp remains. Spoon into blender. Blend
until smooth. Seal in sterilized jars or freeze.

Creole Sauce

28-oz. can	tomato	800-g can
1 medium	onion (chopped)	1 medium
1	green pepper	1
1 t.	paprika	5 mL
¼ t.	marjoram	2 mL
	salt and pepper to taste	

Combine all ingredients and cook over low heat for 25 minutes.

Yield: 2 c. (500 mL)
Exchange: 1 vegetable
Calories: 25

Italian Tomato Sauce

6	tomatoes (peeled and cubed)	6
¼ c.	green pepper (chopped)	60 mL
¼ c.	onion (chopped)	60 mL
2 T.	parsley (chopped)	30 mL
1 T.	lemon juice	15 mL
dash each	oregano, marjoram, thyme, crushed bay leaf, horseradish	dash each
	salt and pepper to taste	

Combine all ingredients in blender. Whip until smooth. Add enough water to make 2 c. (500 mL).

Yield: 2 c. (500 mL)
Exchange: 2 vegetable
Calories: 10

Chili Sauce

28-oz. can	tomatoes	800-g can
1 medium	apple	1 medium
1 medium	onion	1 medium
1 small	green pepper	1 small
1 c.	wine vinegar	250 mL
½ c.	sugar replacement	125 mL
1 T.	salt	15 mL
½ t.	ground clove	3 mL
½ t.	cinnamon	3 mL
½ t.	nutmeg	3 mL

Mash tomatoes; pour into kettle. Grind together apple, onion, green pepper, and vinegar. Add to kettle; cook until thick. Remove from heat. Add sugar replacement and seasonings. Return to heat; cook 5 minutes, stirring constantly.

Yield: 2 c. (500 mL)
Exchange ½ c. (125 mL): 1 fruit
Calories ½ c. (125 mL):   45

Variations for Italian Dressing

To ½ c. (125 mL) lo-cal Italian dressing, add:

Anchovy

Mash 1 oz. (30 g) anchovy fillets.
Exchange: 1 meat

Bacon

Grind 1 T. (15 mL) Bacos; allow to mellow several hours.
Exchange: ½ fat

Parmesan

Add 1 T. (15 mL) Parmesan cheese; allow to mellow several hours.
Exchange: ⅛ meat

Tomato

Add 1 T. (15 mL) tomato puree.

Wine

Add 1 T. (15 mL) dry white or red wine.

Calories ½ c. (125 mL): 24

Variations for French Dressing

To ½ c. (125 mL) lo-cal French dressing, add:

Avocado

Mash avocado to make 2 T. (30 mL)
Exchange: 1 fat

Cheese

Mash Bleu cheese or Roquefort cheese to make 2 T. (30 mL)
Exchange: ¼ meat

Egg

Crumble 1 hard-cooked egg yolk; combine with dash of hot pepper sauce.
Exchange: 1 meat

Lemon

Add 1 T. (15 mL) lemon juice.

Soy Sauce

Add 1 T. (15 mL) soy sauce.

Calories ½ c. (125 mL): 100

Variations for Bleu Cheese Dressing

To ½ c. (125 mL) lo-cal bleu cheese dressing, add:

Anchovy

Mash 1 oz. (30 g) anchovy fillets.
Exchange: 1 meat

Bacon

Grind 1 T. (15 mL) Bacos; allow to mellow several hours.
Exchange: ½ fat

Chive

Chop chives to make 2 T. (30 mL); allow to mellow several hours.

Herb

Combine 1 t. (5 mL) each ground parsley, chives, and marjoram.

Calories ½ c. (125 mL): 56

Salad Dressing

1½ c.	cold water	375 mL
¼ c.	vinegar	60 mL
1½ t.	salt	7 mL
1 t.	yellow mustard	5 mL
2 T.	flour	30 mL
1	egg (well beaten)	1
¼ c.	sugar replacement	60 mL
2 t.	margarine	10 mL

Combine cold water, vinegar, salt, mustard, flour, and egg in top of double boiler. Stir to blend. Cook until thick. Remove from heat. Add sugar replacement and margarine. Stir to blend.

Yield: 1 c. (250 mL)
Exchange 2 T. (30 mL): ½ vegetable
½ fat
Calories 2 T. (30 mL): 31

Sweet Yogurt Dressing

1 c.	lo-cal yogurt	250 mL
½ t.	mace	2 mL
2 t.	sugar replacement	10 mL
dash	salt	dash
½ c.	lo-cal whipped topping (prepared)	125 mL

Drain yogurt; beat until smooth and fluffy. Add mace, sugar replacement, and salt. Beat until blended. Fold in prepared whipped topping. Place in refrigerator until ready to serve. Good on fruit or gelatin salads.

Yield: 1 c. (250 mL)
Exchange: 1 milk
Calories: 100

Herb Yogurt Dressing

1 c.	lo-cal yogurt	250 mL
2 T.	vinegar	30 mL
1 t.	onion (grated)	5 mL
1 t.	celery seeds	5 mL
1 t.	dry mustard	5 mL
1 t.	salt	5 mL
½ t.	thyme	2 mL
	salt and pepper to taste	

Beat yogurt until smooth. Add remaining ingredients; blend well. Cover. Allow to rest at least 1-hour before serving.

Yield: 1 c. (250 mL)
Exchange: 1 milk
Calories: 86

Bay Salad Dressing

3 T.	liquid shortening	45 mL
½ c.	onion (finely chopped)	125 mL
2 T.	fresh parsley (finely chopped)	30 mL
2 T.	celery with leaves (finely chopped)	30 mL
1	bay leaf	1
dash each	thyme, mace, rosemary	dash each
2 T.	white wine	30 mL
1 c.	yogurt	250 mL
2 T.	skim milk	30 mL
	salt and pepper to taste	

Heat liquid shortening in small skillet. Add onion, parsley, celery, and seasonings. Cook over very low heat, stirring constantly, for 15 minutes. DO NOT ALLOW VEGE-TABLES TO BURN. Set aside to cool. Add wine; stir to mix. Allow to rest 30 minutes. Strain, reserving liquid. Beat yogurt with skim milk. Continue beating, adding wine liquid. Add salt and pepper. Blend.

Yield: 1½ c. (375 mL)
Exchange ¼ c. (60 mL): ½ vegetable
½ fat
Calories ¼ c. (60 mL): 44

Tangy Barbecue Sauce

1 c.	Chili Sauce (p. 129)	250 mL
2 T.	lemon juice	30 mL
1 T.	Worcestershire sauce	15 mL
1 t.	horseradish	5 mL
1 t.	Dijon mustard	5 mL
1 T.	brown sugar replacement	15 mL
dash each	hot pepper sauce, soy sauce, salt, pepper	dash each

Combine all ingredients; stir to blend well.

Yield: 1 c. (250 mL)
Exchange: 2 fruit
Calories: 90

Hollandaise Sauce

1	egg yolk	1
1 T.	evaporated (regular or skim) milk	15 mL
⅛ t.	salt	1 mL
dash	cayenne pepper	dash
1 T.	lemon juice	15 mL
1 T.	margarine	15 mL

In the top of a double boiler, heat egg yolk, evaporated milk, salt, and cayenne pepper until thick. Place over hot water. Beat lemon juice into egg mixture until thick and creamy. Remove double boiler from heat. Add margarine, 1 t. (5 mL) at a time. Beat until margarine is melted and blended in.

Yield: ½ c. (125 mL)
Exchange: ½ high-fat meat
3 fat
Calories: 213

White Sauce

2 T.	margarine	30 mL
1½ T.	flour	25 mL
¼ t.	salt	1 mL
1 t.	Worcestershire sauce	5 mL
1 c.	skim milk	250 mL

Melt margarine. Add flour, salt, and Worcestershire sauce. Blend thoroughly. Add skim milk. Cook until slightly thickened.

Yield: 1 c. (250 mL)
Exchange ½ c. (125 mL): 1 bread
½ high-fat meat
Calories ½ c. (125 mL): 190

Orange Sauce

½ t.	cornstarch	2 mL
2 T.	cold water	30 mL
½ c.	orange juice concentrate	125 mL
2 t.	unsweetened orange drink mix	10 mL

Dissolve cornstarch in cold water. Add orange juice concentrate and drink mix. Cook over low heat until slightly thickened. Use as glaze on poultry or pork.

Yield: ½ c. (125 mL)
Exchange: 1 fruit
Calories: 52

Teriyaki Marinade

⅓ c.	soya sauce	80 mL
2 T.	wine vinegar	30 mL
2 T.	sugar replacement	30 mL
2 t.	salt	10 mL
1 t.	ginger (powdered)	5 mL
½ t.	garlic powder	2 mL

Blend well. No calories.

SANDWICH SPREADS AND SNACKS

Beef Tongue Spread

6 oz.	cooked beef tongue (chopped)	180 g
2 T.	Chili Sauce (p. 129)	30 mL
1 T.	onion (finely chopped)	15 mL

Combine all ingredients; blend well.

Yield: 1 c. (250 mL)
Exchange ¼ c. (60 mL): 1 medium-fat meat
Calories ¼ c. (60 mL): 76

Sweet Spread

½ c.	margarine	125 mL
1 t.	cinnamon	5 mL
1 t.	orange rind (grated)	5 mL
½ t.	nutmeg	2 mL
2 T.	sugar replacement	30 mL

Have margarine at room temperature. Beat until light and fluffy. Add remaining ingredients. Beat until blended.

Yield: 24 servings
Exchange 1 t. (5 mL): 1 fat
Calories 1 t. (5 mL): 45

Waldorf Sandwich Spread

¼ c.	celery (finely chopped)	60 mL
1 small	apple (finely chopped)	1 small
1 T.	raisins (finely chopped)	15 mL
6 halves	walnuts (finely chopped)	6 halves
2 T.	Salad Dressing (p. 131)	30 mL
	salt to taste	

Combine all ingredients; blend well.

Yield: ½ c. (125 mL)
Exchange ¼ c. (60 mL): 1 fruit
1 fat
Calories ¼ c. (60 mL): 96

Tacos

3 oz.	lean ground beef	90 g
	salt and pepper to taste	
1 T.	taco sauce	15 mL
3	6-in. (15-cm) taco shells	3
1½ oz.	Cheddar cheese (grated)	45 g
1½ T.	onion (chopped)	25 mL
1 medium	tomato (chopped)	1 medium
1 c.	lettuce (shredded)	250 mL

Brown beef over low heat. Add salt and pepper. Drain. Add taco sauce; mix well. Divide beef mixture evenly among warm crisp shells. Top with cheese, onion, tomato, and lettuce.

Yield: 1 serving
Exchange: 1 bread
4½ meat
1 vegetable
Calories 1 taco: 145

Tuna Spread

6½-oz. can	tuna (in water)	200-mL can
2 T.	onion (finely chopped)	30 mL
2 T.	celery (finely chopped)	30 mL
1 T.	carrot (finely chopped)	15 mL
¼ c.	lo-cal bleu cheese dressing	60 mL
	salt and pepper to taste	

Drain tuna; chop fine. Add remaining ingredients and mix well.

Yield: 1 c. (250 mL)
Exchange ¼ c. (60 mL): 1 lean meat
Calories ¼ c. (60 mL): 48

Blueberry Preserves

(Strawberry—Raspberry)

1 c.	fresh or frozen blueberries (unsweetened)	250 mL
1 t.	lo-cal pectin	5 mL
1 t.	sugar replacement	5 mL

Place blueberries in top of double boiler. Cook over boiling water until soft and juicy. (Crush berries against sides of double boiler.) Add pectin and sugar replacement. Blend in thoroughly. Cook until medium thick. Preserves can also be made with strawberries or raspberries.

Microwave: Place blueberries in glass bowl. Cook on High for 4 minutes until soft and juicy. (Crush berries against sides of bowl.) Add pectin and sugar. Blend in thoroughly. Cook on High 30 seconds.

Yield: ⅔ c. (180 mL)
Exchange: 1 fruit
Calories: 40

Hamburger Relish

2 qt.	cucumbers (ground)	2 L
2	onions	2
2	green peppers	2
1	red pepper	1
¼ c.	salt	60 mL
2 c.	vinegar	500 mL
1 t.	mustard seeds	5 mL
1 t.	celery seeds	5 mL
1 t.	parsley flakes	5 mL
1 t.	turmeric	5 mL
2 c.	sugar replacement	500 mL

Grind cucumbers, onions, green peppers, and red pepper. Stir in salt. Soak overnight; drain. Combine vinegar, mustard seeds, celery seeds, parsley flakes, and turmeric. Bring to a boil; cook for 10 minutes. Add ground vegetables; cook for 20 minutes. Remove from heat. Add sugar replacement; stir to dissolve. Allow to rest 24 hours; stir often. Drain slightly if too much liquid accumulates. Pack in scalded jars; seal.

Yield: About 5 pints
Exchange 1 T. (15 mL): Negligible
Calories 1 T. (15 mL): Negligible

Beef Jerky

2 lb.	flank steak	1 kg
½ c.	soy sauce	125 mL
	lemon pepper to taste	
	garlic salt to taste	

Thoroughly chill flank steak. Cut into ¼ x 8-in. (6 x 20-cm) strips. Combine soy sauce, lemon pepper, and garlic salt. Marinate steak in sauce for 24 hours; drain. Place on broiler pan. Bake at 150° F (66° C) for 10 to 12 hours, or until dry.

Exchange 2 strips: 1 high-fat meat
Calories 2 strips: 108

Teeny Pizza

	dough for 1 biscuit	
1 T.	Tomato Sauce (p. 128)	30 mL
dash each	garlic powder, oregano, thyme, salt	dash each
½ oz.	meat of your choice	15 g
½ oz.	mozzarella cheese (shredded)	15 g

Press or roll biscuit dough flat. Roll edge up or place in individual baking dish. Combine Tomato Sauce and seasonings. Spread over entire surface of biscuit. Top with meat and cheese. Bake at 450° F (230° C) for 10 minutes.

Yield: 1 serving
Exchange: 1 meat
1 bread
Calories: 150

Wrapped Wiener

1	wiener	1
⅜-in. strip	cheese	1-cm strip
	dough for 1 biscuit	

Make a thin slit in wiener; insert strip of cheese in slit. Roll or pat biscuit dough thin. Place wiener on edge of dough; roll up. Secure by pinching dough together, or use a toothpick. Bake at 375° F (190° C) for 15 minutes, or until golden brown.

Yield: 1 serving
Exchange: 1¼ meat
1 bread
Calories: 141

Fish Bundles

½ c.	Herb-Seasoned Stuffing (p. 97)	125 mL
8 oz.	Cooked Flaked Fish (p. 72)	240 g
1	egg	1

Moisten stuffing with water. Allow to stand 5 minutes, or until soft. (Add extra water if needed.) Blend fish and egg into softened stuffing. Form into 6 patties. Broil for 10 to 15 minutes. Turn once.

Yield: 6 patties
Exchange 1 patty: 1¼ meat
¼ bread
⅛ fat
Calories 1 patty: 45

Garlic Dill Pickles

3 c.	water	750 mL
3 c.	vinegar	750 mL
½ c.	pickling salt	125 mL
	firm medium cucumbers (quartered)	
1 per jar	dill head	1 per jar
1 per jar	garlic clove	1 per jar

Combine water, vinegar, and pickling salt. Bring to a boil; cook for 5 minutes. Divide cucumbers, dill, and garlic among three scalded 1 qt. (1 L) jars. Fill jars with vinegar mixture. Seal immediately. Ready in 6 to 8 weeks.

Exchange 1 pickle: Negligible
Calories 1 pickle: Negligible

Bread and Butter Pickles

4 qt.	cucumbers (sliced)	4 L
5	onions	5
1 qt.	crushed ice	1 L
⅓ c.	salt	90 mL
2 c.	vinegar	500 mL
1½ t.	turmeric	7 mL
1½ t.	celery seeds	7 mL
2 t.	mustard seeds	10 mL
1 t.	ginger	5 mL
1½ c.	sugar replacement	375 mL

Slice cucumbers and onions; place in large saucepan. Mix ice and salt; stir into cucumbers and onions. Cover. Chill for 5 to 6 hours. Drain; remove ice. Combine vinegar and seasonings. Bring to a boil; simmer for 5 minutes. Add sugar replacement; stir to dissolve. Add drained cucumbers and onions. Bring to a boil. Put into scalded jars and seal.

Yield: 4–5 pints
Exchange 1 T. (15 mL): Negligible
Calories 1 T. (15 mL): Negligible

Dill Midgets

1 head	dill	1 head
20–25	firm midget cucumbers	20–25
½ t.	alum	2 mL
2 t.	pickling salt	10 mL
½ c.	white vinegar	125 mL

Scald 1 pt. (½ L) jar. Push dill head to bottom of jar. Fill with midgets. Add alum and pickling salt. Pour vinegar over top. Add enough cold water to fill jar; seal. Shake vigorously. Ready in 8 to 10 weeks.

Yield: 20–25 pickles
Exchange 1 pickle: Negligible
Calories 1 pickle: Negligible

Russian Teasicles

2 qt.	water	2 L
1	cinnamon stick	1
3	whole cloves	3
2 T.	black tea leaves	30 mL
6-oz. can	frozen lemon juice (unsweetened)	180-mL can
6-oz. can	frozen orange juice	180-mL can
½ c.	sugar replacement	125 mL

Combine water, cinnamon stick, whole cloves, and black tea leaves in large kettle. Bring to a boil; reduce heat and simmer for 15 to 20 minutes. Strain; cool slightly. Add frozen concentrates and sugar replacement. Stir to dissolve. Pour into freezer stick trays; freeze.

Yield: about 38 popsicles
Exchange 1 popsicle: ½ fruit
Calories 1 popsicle: 5

Egg Nog

1	egg (well beaten)	1
2 t.	sugar replacement	30 mL
dash	salt, vanilla extract	dash
¾ c.	cold milk	180 mL
dash	nutmeg to taste	dash

Combine egg with sugar replacement and salt. Add vanilla extract and cold milk. Beat well. Pour into glass or mug; sprinkle with nutmeg.

Yield: 1 serving
Exchange: 1 meat
           1 milk
Calories: 148

DESSERTS

Washington's Cherry Pie

9-in.	unbaked pie shell	23-cm
2 c.	unsweetened cherries	500 mL
¼ c.	soft margarine	60 mL
1 T.	flour	15 mL
½ c.	sugar replacement	125 mL
2	egg yolks	2
¼ c.	evaporated milk	60 mL
½ t.	vanilla extract	2 mL
2	egg whites	2
2 t.	granulated sugar replacement	10 mL

Drain cherries; pour into unbaked pie shell. Cream margarine, flour, and sugar replacement. Add egg yolks and beat until smooth. Add evaporated milk and vanilla extract. Pour over cherries. Bake at 450° F (230° C) for 10 minutes. Reduce heat. Bake at 350° F (175° C) for 30 minutes. Whip egg whites until soft peaks form. Add granulated sugar; whip until thick and stiff. Top pie filling with meringue, carefully sealing edges. Bake at 350° F (175° C) for 12 to 15 minutes, or until delicately brown.

Yield: 8 servings
Exchange 1 serving: 1 fruit
1 fat
plus pie shell exchange
Calories 1 serving: 88
plus pie shell calories

Basic Pie Shell

⅓ c.	shortening	90 mL
1 c.	flour	250 mL
¼ t.	salt	1 mL
2 to 4 T.	ice water	30 to 60 mL

Chill shortening. Cut shortening into flour and salt until mixture forms crumbs. Add ice water, 1 T. (15 mL) at a time. Flip mixture around in bowl until a ball forms. Wrap in plastic wrap. Chill at least 1 hour. Roll to fit 9-in. (23-cm) pie pan. Fill with pie filling or prick with fork. Bake at 425° F (220° C) for 10 to 12 minutes or until firm, or leave unbaked.

Yield: 8 servings
Exchange 1 serving: 1 bread
2 fat
Calories 1 serving: 170

Fresh Strawberry Pie

9-in.	baked pie shell	23-cm
1 pkg. (⅝ oz.)	lo-cal strawberry gelatin	1 pkg. (20 g)
1 qt.	fresh strawberries	1 L
1 pkg.	lo-cal whipped topping (prepared)	1 pkg.

Prepare one envelope of gelatin as directed on package. Allow to semi-set. Rinse and hull berries; place in baked pie shell. Pour gelatin over top; chill until firm. Top with prepared whipped topping.

Yield: 8 servings
Exchange 1 serving: ½ fruit
plus pie shell exchange
Calories 1 serving: 20
plus pie shell calories

Fine-Crumb Pie Shell

1¼ c.	fine crumbs (graham cracker, dry cereal, zwieback)	300 mL
3 T.	margarine (melted)	45 mL
1 T.	water	15 mL
	spices (see spice and herb list)	
	sugar replacement	

Combine crumbs with melted margarine and water; add spices and sugar replacement, if desired. Spread evenly in 9-in. (23-cm) pie pan. Press firmly onto sides and bottom. Either chill until set or bake at 325° (165° C) for 8 to 10 minutes.

Yield:	8 servings
Exchange 1 serving Graham Cracker:	1 bread
	1 fat
Calories 1 serving Graham Cracker:	85
Exchange 1 serving Dry Cereal:	½ bread
	1 fat
Calories 1 serving Dry Cereal:	64
Exchange 1 serving Zwieback:	½ bread
	1 fat
Calories 1 serving Zwieback:	70

Blueberry Cream Pie

9-in.	baked pie shell	23-cm
2 c.	lo-cal whipped topping (prepared)	500 mL
1½ c.	Blueberry Topping (p. 148)	375 mL

Fold prepared whipped topping into Blueberry Topping. Spread into baked pie shell. Chill until firm.

Yield:	8 servings
Exchange 1 serving:	½ fruit
	plus pie shell exchange
Calories 1 serving:	30
	plus pie shell calories

Homemade Ice Cream

13-oz. can	evaporated milk	385-mL can
2 T.	sugar replacement	30 mL
1½ c.	whole milk	375 mL
1 T.	vanilla extract	15 mL
3	eggs (well beaten)	3

Combine evaporated milk and sugar replacement. Beat well until sugar is dissolved. Add whole milk and vanilla extract; beat well. Add eggs; beat eggs into milk mixture vigorously. Pour into ice cream maker. Freeze according to manufacturer's directions.

Yield: 8 servings
Exchange 1 serving: ½ milk
½ lean meat
Calories 1 serving: 122

Cranberry-Pineapple Pie

9-in.	unbaked pie shell	23-cm
1½ c.	unsweetened crushed pineapple	375 mL
½ c.	sugar replacement	125 mL
1 T.	cornstarch	15 mL
½ t.	salt	2 mL
1 T.	butter	15 mL
2 c.	cranberries	500 mL

Drain pineapple; reserve liquid. Blend ½ c. (125 mL) of the pineapple liquid with cornstarch. Cook until very thick. Stir in sugar replacement, salt and butter. Add cranberries and drained pineapple. Pour into unbaked pie shell. Bake at 425° F (220° C) for 30 to 40 minutes, or until set.

Yield: 8 servings
Exchange 1 serving: 1 fruit
½ fat
plus pie shell exchange
Calories 1 serving: 30
plus pie shell calories

Fudge Candy

13-oz. can	evaporated milk	385-mL can
3 T.	cocoa	45 mL
¼ c.	butter	60 mL
1 T.	sugar replacement	15 mL
dash	salt	dash
1 t.	vanilla extract	5 mL
2½ c.	unsweetened cereal crumbs	625 mL
¼ c.	nuts (very finely chopped)	60 mL

Combine evaporated milk and cocoa in saucepan. Cook and beat over low heat until cocoa is dissolved. Add butter, sugar replacement, salt, and vanilla extract. Bring to a boil; reduce heat. Cook for 2 minutes. Remove from heat; add cereal crumbs and work in with wooden spoon. Cool 15 minutes. Divide in half; roll each half into a tube, 8 in. (20 cm) long. Roll tubes in finely chopped nuts. Wrap in waxed paper; chill overnight. Cut in ¼-in. (6-mm) slices.

Yield: 64 slices
Exchange 2 slices: ½ bread
½ fat
Calories 2 slices: 60

Jell Jells

1 qt.	lo-cal orange soda	1 L
4 env.	unflavored gelatin	4 env.
1½ pkg. (⅝ oz.)	lo-cal orange gelatin	1½ pkg. (20 g)

Bring orange soda to a boil. Combine gelatins together in large bowl; add boiling water. Stir to dissolve. Pour into pan. Chill until firm. Cut into cubes.

Exchange: Negligible
Calories: Negligible

Strawberry Cream Pie

9-in.	baked pie shell	23-cm
1 pkg.	lo-cal vanilla pudding	1 pkg.
1½ c.	Strawberry Topping (p. 148)	375 mL
¼ c.	fresh strawberries (halved)	60 mL
1 pkg.	lo-cal whipped topping (prepared)	1 pkg.

Prepare pudding as directed on package; cool slightly. Pour into baked pie shell. Cover with waxed paper; chill until set. Combine Strawberry Topping with fresh strawberries. Spread evenly on top of pudding. Top with prepared whipped topping.

Yield: 8 servings
Exchange 1 serving: 1½ fruit
½ milk
plus pie shell exchange
Calories 1 serving: 75
plus pie shell calories

Strawberry Topping
(Blueberry—Raspberry)

2 c.	fresh or frozen strawberries (unsweetened)	500 mL
1½ t.	cornstarch	7 mL
¼ c.	cold water	60 mL
2 t.	sugar replacement	10 mL

Place strawberries in top of double boiler. Cook over boiling water until soft and juicy. Blend cornstarch and cold water. Add to strawberries. Cook until clear and slightly thickened. Remove from heat; add sugar replacement. Cool. Topping can also be made with blueberries or raspberries.

Yield: 1½ c. (375 mL)
Exchange ½ c. (125 mL): 1 fruit
Calories ½ c. (125 mL): 40

Strawberry Shortcake

	dough for 1 biscuit	
½ c.	Strawberry Topping (p. 148)	125 mL
¼ c.	fresh strawberries (halved)	60 mL
2 T.	lo-cal whipped topping (prepared)	30 mL

Bake biscuit as directed on package. Cool. Cut in half. Layer biscuit, half of the Strawberry Topping, and half of the strawberries; repeat. Top with prepared whipped topping.

Yield: 1 serving
Exchange: 1 bread
          1½ fruit
Calories: 100

Lemon Ice Freeze

1 env.	unflavored gelatin	1 env.
1½ c.	milk	375 mL
2	egg yolks (slightly beaten)	2
¼ t.	salt	2 mL
½ c.	sugar replacement	125 mL
2 t.	lemon extract	10 mL
2 T.	lemon peel	30 mL
2	egg whites (stiffly beaten)	2

Soften gelatin in ¼ c. (60 mL) of the milk; set aside. Combine egg yolks, remaining milk, salt, sugar replacement, lemon extract and peel in top of double boiler. Cook until thick and creamy. Remove from heat. Add gelatin mixture; stir until dissolved. Cool. Pour into ice cube tray and freeze. Place mixture in cold bowl and beat until smooth; fold in stiffly beaten egg whites. Return to tray and refreeze.

Yield: 6 servings
Exchange 1 serving: ½ milk exchange
               ⅓ meat
Calories 1 serving: 100

Lemon Cake Pie

9-in.	unbaked pie shell	23-cm
½ c.	sugar replacement	125 mL
2 T.	flour	30 mL
2 T.	margarine (soft)	30 mL
1 T.	lemon rind	15 mL
3 T.	lemon juice	45 mL
1 c.	skim milk	250 mL
2	eggs, separated	2

Combine sugar replacement, flour, margarine, lemon rind and juice, skim milk, and egg yolks. Beat vigorously. Fold in egg whites (well beaten). Pour into unbaked pie shell. Bake at 325° F (165° C) for 1 hour, or until set.

Yield: 8 servings
Exchange 1 serving: 1 milk
plus pie shell exchange
Calories 1 serving: 40
plus pie shell calories

Fresh Rhubarb Pie

9-in.	unbaked pie shell	23-cm
1 qt.	1-in. (2.5-cm) pieces rhubarb	1 L
4 T.	flour	60 mL
½ c.	sugar replacement	125 mL
2	eggs (beaten)	2

Mix rhubarb, flour, sugar replacement, and eggs. Pour into unbaked pie shell. Bake at 350° F (175° C) for 40 to 50 minutes, or until set.

Yield: 8 servings
Exchange 1 serving: ½ fruit
plus pie shell exchange
Calories 1 serving: 68
plus pie shell calories

Apple-Go-Round

1 firm	apple	1 firm
¼ c.	orange juice	60 mL
1 t.	lemon juice	5 mL
1 T.	raisins	15 mL
1 T.	celery (diced)	15 mL
2 T.	applesauce	30 mL
	lettuce leaf	

Slice off top of apple; remove core. Prick outside with sharp fork. Place apple in tall narrow bowl. Combine orange and lemon juice; pour over apple. (Add extra water if apple is not covered.) Marinate in refrigerator 4 to 5 hours. Combine raisins, celery, and applesauce. Allow to mellow at room temperature 2 hours. Chill thoroughly. Drain apple. Cut apple into 8 sections, slicing almost to the bottom. Fill with applesauce mixture. Place on crisp lettuce leaf.

Yield: 1 serving
Exchange: 2 fruit
Calories: 54

Peach Melba

½ c.	raspberries	125 mL
½ t.	sugar replacement	5 mL
½ c.	dietetic vanilla ice cream	125 ml
½	peach (sliced)	½

Slightly mash raspberries and sugar replacement. Allow to rest 5 minutes. Place ice cream in dish. Top with peach slices and raspberries.

Yield: 1 serving
Exchange: 1 bread
           1 fruit
Calories: 120

Rhubarb Pudding

1 qt.	rhubarb (cut in pieces)	1 L
1 c.	water	250 mL
2 T.	cornstarch	30 mL
1 t.	sugar replacement	5 mL

Cut rhubarb into pieces. Place rhubarb in saucepan. Add water. Cook rhubarb until tender. Mix cornstarch with small amount of cold water; add to rhubarb. Cook until thickened. Remove from heat; add sugar replacement. Stir until dissolved.

Microwave: Place rhubarb in large bowl. Add water. Cook on High for 4 minutes, or until tender. Mix cornstarch with small amount of cold water; add to rhubarb. Cook on High for 1 to 2 minutes, or until thickened.

Yield: 6 servings
Exchange 1 serving: ⅛ fruit
⅛ bread
Calories 1 serving: 22

Banana Cake Roll

4	eggs (separated)	4
10 T.	granulated sugar replacement	150 mL
½ t.	vanilla extract	2 mL
⅔ c.	cake flour (sifted)	180 mL
1 t.	baking powder	5 mL
¼ t.	salt	1 mL
	vegetable cooking spray	
1 pkg.	lo-cal banana pudding (prepared)	1 pkg.
	Chocolate Drizzle (p. 153)	

Beat egg yolks until thick and lemon colored; gradually beat in 3 T. (45 mL) of the sugar replacement. Add vanilla extract. Beat egg whites to soft peaks; gradually beat in the remaining sugar replacement; beat until stiff peaks form. Fold yolks into whites. Sift together cake flour, baking powder, and salt. Fold into egg mixture. Spread batter into 15½ x 10½ x 1-in. (39 x 25 x 3-cm) jelly-roll pan (coated with vegetable cooking spray and lightly floured). Bake at 375° F (190° C) for 10 to 15 minutes, or until done. Loosen sides and turn out on towel lightly sprinkled with a mixture of flour and sugar replacement. Roll up cake and towel from narrow end. Cool completely; unroll. Spread evenly with prepared banana pudding. Roll up. Frost with Chocolate Drizzle.

Yield: 10 servings
Exchange 1 serving: 1 bread
½ fruit
¼ milk
Calories 1 serving: 62

Chocolate Drizzle

2 t.	cornstarch	10 mL
¼ c.	cold water	60 mL
dash	salt	dash
1 oz.	unsweetened chocolate	30 g
⅓ c.	sugar replacement	90 mL
½ t.	butter	3 mL

Blend cornstarch and cold water. Pour into small saucepan. Add salt and chocolate. Cook on low heat until chocolate melts and mixture is thick. Remove from heat. Stir in sugar replacement. Blend in butter.

Yield: ⅓ c. (90 mL)
Exchange: Negligible
Calories: Negligible

Raisin Rice Pudding

1 pkg.	lo-cal rice pudding	1 pkg.
½ c.	raisins	125 mL

Prepare rice pudding as directed on package. Soak raisins in warm water for 1 hour. Drain thoroughly. Add raisins to rice pudding.

Yield: 5 servings, ½ c. (125 mL each)

Exchange 1 serving: ½ bread
½ milk
½ fruit

Calories 1 serving: 100

Brownies

½ c.	flour	125 mL
½ t.	baking powder	2 mL
½ t.	salt	2 mL
3 oz.	unsweetened chocolate (melted)	90 g
½ c.	shortening (soft)	125 mL
2	eggs (beaten)	2
2 T.	granulated sugar	30 mL
1½ c.	sugar replacement	375 mL
1 t.	vanilla extract	5 mL

Combine all ingredients. Beat vigorously until well blended. Spread mixture into greased 8-in.- (20-cm-) square pan. Bake at 350° F (175° C) for 30 to 35 minutes. Cut into 2-in. (5-cm) squares.

Microwave: Cook on Medium for 8 to 10 minutes, or until puffed and dry on top. Cut into 2-in. (5-cm) squares.

Yield: 16 brownies

Exchange 1 brownie: 1½ bread
1½ fat

Calories 1 brownie: 136

Cranberry Bars

1¼ c.	flour	300 mL
1 c.	cereal crumbs	250 mL
¼ t.	salt	1 mL
¼ c.	cold butter	60 mL
1	egg (beaten)	1
4 T.	sugar replacement	60 mL
2 T.	nuts	30 mL
	vegetable cooking spray	
1	orange	1
1½ c.	cranberries	375 mL
⅓ c.	water	60 mL
2 T.	cornstarch	30 mL
½ t.	ground allspice	2 mL

Combine flour, cereal crumbs, and salt in mixing bowl. Cut in cold butter until mixture resembles cornmeal. Combine egg and 1 T. (15 mL) of the sugar replacement. Toss with fork until well blended. Combine 1 c. (250 mL) of the crumb mixture with nuts; reserve for topping. Press remaining crumb mixture into bottom of 8-in.- (20-cm-) square pan coated with vegetable cooking spray. Squeeze orange; reserve ⅓ c. (90 mL) of the juice. Grind the rest of the orange (except for seeds) with cranberries. Combine reserved orange juice, water, 3 T. (45 mL) of the sugar replacement, cornstarch, and allspice. Stir in cranberry-orange mixture. Cook over medium heat until thick and clear, stirring frequently. Spread over crumb crust; sprinkle with reserved nut-crumb mixture. Bake at 350° F (175° C) for 25 minutes. Cool. Cut into 2-in. (5-cm) squares.

Yield: 16 bars
Exchange 1 bar: 1 vegetable
1 fat
½ fruit
Calories 1 bar: 92

Oatmeal Cookies

1 c.	flour	250 mL
½ t.	salt	2 mL
½ t.	baking powder	2 mL
¼ t.	baking soda	2 mL
½ t.	cinnamon	3 mL
½ t.	nutmeg	2 mL
½ c.	raisins	125 mL
1½ c.	oatmeal	375 mL
½ c.	sugar replacement	125 mL
½ c.	margarine (melted)	125 mL
1	egg	1
½ c.	skim milk	125 mL

Combine flour, salt, baking powder, baking soda, cinnamon, nutmeg, raisins, and oatmeal. Mix thoroughly. Beat in sugar replacement, melted margarine, egg, and skim milk. (Add small amount of water if dough is too stiff.) Drop by teaspoonfuls onto cookie sheet. Bake at 400° F (200° C) for 10 minutes.

Yield: 36 cookies
Exchange 1 cookie: ½ bread
¼ fat
Calories 1 cookie: 37

Strawberry Turnovers

¼ t.	cornstarch	2 mL
1 T.	water	15 mL
½ c.	Strawberry Topping (p. 148)	125 mL
1	dough for Basic Pie Shell (p. 144)	1
	Vanilla Gloss (p. 158)	

Blend cornstarch and water. Add to Strawberry Topping. Cook over low heat until very thick. Roll pie dough thin. Cut into eight 4-in. (10-cm) squares. Place 1½ t. (7 mL) of the strawberry mixture into center of each square. Fold each square into a triangle; press sides securely together to seal. Bake at 400° F (200° C) for 9 to 11 minutes, or until golden brown. Brush with Vanilla Gloss.

Microwave: Use microwave only for strawberry filling. Blend cornstarch and water. Add to Strawberry Topping. Cook on High for 30 seconds, or until very thick. Proceed as above.

Yield: 8 turnovers
Exchange 1 turnover: 1 bread
Calories 1 turnover: 180

Baked Apple Dumpling

1 t.	raisins	5 mL
2 T.	orange juice	30 mL
½ t.	sugar replacement	3 mL
1 small	apple	1 small
	dough for 1 biscuit	

Combine raisins and orange juice in saucepan. Heat to a boil. Add sugar replacement. Cover. Allow to rest while preparing remaining ingredients. Core apple; with a fork or toothpick, prick inside the apple cavity. On floured board, roll biscuit dough very thin and large enough to wrap around apple. Place apple in center of dough. Fill apple cavity with raisin mixture. Wrap dough around apple and secure at top. Place in baking dish. Bake at 375° F (190° C) for 25 to 30 minutes.

Yield: 1 serving
Exchange: 1 bread
1 fruit
Calories: 142

Chocolate Topping

3 c.	skim milk	750 mL
2 oz.	unsweetened chocolate	60 g
3 T.	cornstarch	45 mL
½ c.	sugar replacement	125 mL
1 t.	salt	5 mL
2 T.	butter	30 mL
2 t.	vanilla extract	10 mL

Combine skim milk, chocolate, cornstarch, sugar replacement, and salt in saucepan. Bring to a full boil. Boil for 2 to 3 minutes; remove from heat. Add butter and vanilla extract.

Yield: 3 c. (750 mL)
Exchange 2 T. (30 mL): ½ bread
½ fat
Calories 2 T. (30 mL): 35

Vanilla Gloss

¼ c.	cold water	60 mL
2 t.	cornstarch	10 mL
dash	salt	dash
⅓ c.	sugar replacement	90 mL
1 t.	vanilla extract	5 mL

Blend cold water and cornstarch. Pour into small saucepan. Add salt. Boil until clear and thickened. Remove from heat. Add sugar replacement and vanilla extract. Stir to dissolve. Cool.

Yield: ¼ c. (60 mL)
Exchange: Negligible
Calories: Negligible

FOOD EXCHANGE LISTS

Your Diet and the Big Six

A diabetic's diet is multi-purpose. First, it is to keep you in good health; second, to keep the disease under control. Perhaps it would be easier to understand the individual nutritional needs if we understood what happens to food after it is swallowed. The body uses the three energy elements from food to: 1) develop heat and energy from carbohydrates; 2) develop new muscle and blood tissue from protein; 3) develop protective covering for organs from fat. Because the diabetic cannot digest and metabolize food the same way the non-diabetic can, the American Diabetes Association has developed an "Exchange List" for foods.

The Exchange Lists are grouped into six basic food groups: Milk, Vegetable, Fruit, Bread, Meat, and Fat. Food in any one group or exchange may be substituted for any other food in the same group or exchange; all foods within the same group or exchange have approximately the same grams of carbohydrates, proteins, fats, and calorie values. By picking and choosing from the Exchange List, it's easy to develop meals that are both tasty and appealing to you as an individual.

Suppose your doctor or diet counselor has told you that for breakfast you should have the following exchanges:

1 fruit
2 bread
2 meat
1 milk
1 fat

By referring to the Exchange List, you could make up a breakfast something like this:

4 oz. (125 mL) orange juice	1 fruit
1 toasted English muffin	2 bread
2 eggs	2 meat
8 oz. (250 mL) milk	1 milk
1 t. (5 mL) margarine or butter	1 fat
or	
½ grapefruit	1 fruit
¾ c. (190 mL) puffed or flaked cereal	1 bread
1 piece of toast	1 bread
2 oz. (60 g) Canadian bacon	2 meat
8 oz. (250 mL) milk	1 milk
1 t. (5 mL) margarine or butter	1 fat
or	
¼ cantaloupe	1 fruit
1 c. (250 mL) cooked rice	2 bread
2 oz. (60 g) pork sausage	2 meat
8 oz. (250 mL) milk	1 milk
1 t. (5 mL) margarine or butter	1 fat
or	
¾ c. (190 mL) strawberries blended with 1 c. (250 mL) yogurt	1 fruit / 1 milk
Small cheese omelet	2 meat
2 pieces of toast	2 bread
1 t. (5 mL) margarine or butter	1 fat

As you can see, there is a wide selection open to you. When you start planning your meals, remember to ask your doctor or diet counselor if you have any questions—never guess on your own.

Milk Exchange

NON-FAT: One exchange contains 12 grams carbohydrates, 8 grams protein, and 80 calories.

Non-fat milk (skim, buttermilk, plain yogurt)	1 c. (250 mL)
Non-fat canned	½ c. (125 mL)
Non-fat powdered solids	⅓ c. (90 mL)

LOW-FAT: One exchange contains 12 grams carbohydrates, 8 grams protein, 5 grams fat, and 125 calories.

1%; omit ½ fat exchange	1 c. (250 mL)
2% milk; omit 1 fat exchange	1 c. (250 mL)
2% yogurt; omit 1 fat exchange	1 c. (250 mL)

FULL-FAT: One exchange contains 12 grams carbohydrates, 8 grams protein, 10 grams fat, and 170 calories; omit 2 fat exchanges.

Whole milk, buttermilk, plain yogurt	1 c. (250 mL)
Canned whole milk	½ c. (125 mL)

Vegetable Exchange

One exchange, cooked without fat, contains 5 grams carbohydrates, 2 grams protein, and 25 calories. One exchange is ½ c. (125 mL), cooked.

Asparagus	Mushrooms
Bamboo Shoots	Onions
Bean Sprouts	Rutabaga
Broccoli	Sauerkraut
Brussels Sprouts	String Beans (Green and Yellow)
Cabbage	Summer Squash
Cauliflower	Tomatoes
Celery	Tomato Juice
Eggplant	Turnips
Green Pepper	Zucchini

Cooked Greens: **One** exchange is ½ c. (125 mL) cooked.

Beet	Mustard
Chard	Spinach
Dandelion	Turnip

The following vegetables, eaten raw, may be used as desired.

Bean Sprouts	Cucumbers	Parsley
Cauliflower	Endive	Radishes
Celery	Escarole	Watercress
Chicory	Lettuce	
Chinese Cabbage	Mushrooms	

Starchy vegetables are on the Bread Exchange.

Fruit Exchange

Fruit and juices should not contain sugar. Sugar substitutes may be added, if desired. One exchange contains 10 grams carbohydrates and 40 calories.

Apples	1 small
Applesauce	½ c. (125 mL)
Apricots	2 medium
Banana	½ small
Berries:	
Blackberries	½ c. (125 mL)
Blueberries	½ c. (125 mL)
Cherries	10 large
Raspberries	½ c. (125 mL)
Strawberries	¾ c. (190 mL)
Citrus Fruits:	
Grapefruit	½ small
Lemon	as desired
Lime	as desired
Orange	1 small
Nectarine	1 medium
Tangerine	1 medium
Cranberries	as desired

Dried Fruits:

Apples	2 halves
Apricots	4 halves
Figs	1
Peaches	2 halves
Pears	2 halves
Prunes	2 medium
Raisins	2 T. (30 mL)
Grapes	12

Juices:

Apple juice or cider	⅓ c. (90 mL)
Cranberry (no sugar)	as desired
Grapefruit	½ c. (125 mL)
Grape	¼ c. (60 mL)
Orange	½ c. (125 mL)
Pineapple	⅓ c. (90 mL)
Prune	¼ c. (60 mL)
Tangerine	½ c. (125 mL)
Peach	1 medium
Pear	1 medium
Pineapple	½ c. (125 mL)
Plums	2 medium

Bread Exchange

One exchange contains 15 grams carbohydrate, 2 grams protein, and 70 calories.

Bagel	½ small
Bread:	
White (including French and Italian)	1 slice
Whole or Cracked Wheat	1 slice
Rye or Pumpernickel	1 slice
Raisin	1 slice
Party Rye	3 small rounds
Pita	¼ slice

Bread (cont'd):

Thin Slice (White or Dark)	1½ slices
Hollywood	2 slices
Cornbread, 2-in. (5-cm) square; omit 1 fat exchange	1 slice
Boston Brown 3 x ½-in. (5 x 1-cm)	1 slice
Dinner Roll	1 small
English Muffin	½ small
Plain Muffin; omit 1 fat exchange	1
Biscuit, 2-in. (5-cm); omit 1 fat exchange	1
Sandwich Roll or Bun	1
Bread Croutons	1 c. (250 mL)
Bread Stick, 8 x ½-in. (20 x 1½-cm)	2
Bread Stick, 4 x ¼-in. (10-cm x 5-mm)	6
Tortilla or Taco Shell, 6-in. (15-cm)	3
Bread Crumbs (fine)	¼ c. (60 mL)
Gingerbread, 2-in. (5-cm); omit 1 fat exchange	1
Bread Stuffing; omit 1 fat exchange	½ c. (125 mL)
Toast, Melba	4 oblong, or 8 round
Cake, pound, 3 x 3 x ½-in. (8 x 8 x 1-cm); omit 1 fat exchange	1
Cake, sponge or angel food, 1½-in. (1-cm) cube	1
Cereal:	
Bran or Bran Buds	¼ c. (60 mL)
Bran Flakes	½ c. (125 mL)
Unsweetened Cereal	¾ c. (180 mL)
Unsweetened Puff Cereal	1 c. (250 mL)
Cooked Cereals	½ c. (125 mL)
Chinese Noodles	½ c. (125 mL)
Cookies:	
Vanilla wafers	5

Cookies (cont'd):

Gingersnaps	5
Lorna Doon Shortbread	3
Fig Newton, ½ oz. (15 g)	1
Plain, 3-in. (8-cm)	1
Oreo Sandwich; omit 1 fat exchange	2

Crackers:

Animal	8
Arrowroot	3
Bugles; omit 2 fat exchanges	30
Doo Dads; omit 1 fat exchange	¾ c. (180 mL)
Holland Rusks	2
Graham, 2½-in. (7-cm) square	2
Multi-shaped; omit 1 fat exchange	11
Matzoth 4 x 6-in. (2 x 3-cm)	½
Ritz, Hi Ho, etc.	6 rounds
Onion-flavored; omit 1 fat exchange	10
Oyster	20
Cheese Nips Tidbits	60
Cheese; omit 1 fat exchange	6 rounds
Ry Krisp	3
Shredded Wheat Wafers	3
Thin Triangle; omit 1 fat exchange	14
Saltines, 2-in. (5-cm) square	5
Triscuit	5
Wheat Thins	10
Whistles; omit 1 fat exchange	30

Cream Puff Shell; omit 1 fat exchange	1 small
Doughnut, plain; omit 2 fat exchanges	1

Ice Cream:

Chocolate; omit 2 fat exchanges	½ c. (125 mL)
Vanilla; omit 2 fat exchanges	½ c. (125 mL)
Strawberry; omit 2 fat exchanges	½ c. (125 mL)
Dairy Queen; omit 1 fat exchange	⅓ c. (90 mL)
Marshmallows	3 large

Popcorn (unbuttered)	1 c. (250 mL)
Pretzels	20 thin, or 6 twists

Vegetables:

Dried Beans, Peas, Lentils	½ c. (125 mL)
Corn	⅓ c. (60 mL)
Corn on the Cob	1 small
Beets	½ c. (125 mL)
Carrots	½ c. (125 mL)
Onions	½ c. (125 mL)
Peas	½ c. (125 mL)
Potato	1 small
Potato Chips; omit 2 fat exchanges	15, or 1 oz. (30 g) bag
Potatoes, Shoestring; omit 2 fat exchanges	⅔ c. (300 g)
Pumpkin	1 c. (250 mL)
Rutabaga	½ c. (125 mL)
Tomato Sauce	½ c. (125 mL)
Tomato Paste	¼ c. (60 mL)
Winter Squash	½ c. (125 mL)

Waffle, 4-in. (10-cm) square; omit 1 fat exchange	1
Zwieback	3

Meat Exchange

LEAN MEAT: One exchange contains 7 grams protein, 3 grams fat, and 55 calories.

Beef: chipped beef, chuck, flank, round and tenderloin steaks, all cuts rump and sirloin	1 oz. (30 g)
Lamb: any lean, trimmed cut	1 oz. (30 g)
Veal: any lean, trimmed cut	1 oz. (30 g)
Poultry (without skin): chicken, turkey, Cornish hen, pheasant	1 oz. (30 g)

Fish and seafood: any fresh or frozen	1 oz. (30 g)
Canned fish or seafood: packed in water	¼ c. (60 mL)

MEDIUM-FAT MEAT: One exchange contains 7 grams protein, 6 grams fat, and 78 calories.

Beef: ground beef (15% fat)	1 oz. (30 g)
Pork: loin shoulder and leg cuts, ham, Canadian bacon, Boston butt	1 oz. (30 g)
Egg	1
Cheese: white	1 oz. (30 g)
Cottage cheese	¼ c. (60 mL)

HIGH-FAT MEAT: One exchange contains 7 grams protein, 8 grams fat, and 100 calories.

Beef: ground beef (20% fat), brisket, rib and club cuts	1 oz. (30 g)
Pork: ground pork, rib cuts	1 oz. (30 g)
Poultry: duck, goose, capons	1 oz. (30 g)
Cheese: cheddar type	1 oz. (30 g)
Cold cuts and wieners	1

Fat Exchange

One exchange contains 5 grams fat and 45 calories.

Margarine or butter	1 t. (5 mL)
Bacon, crisp	1 slice
Cream, light (20%)	2 T. (30 mL)
heavy (40%)	1 T. (15 mL)
sour	2 T. (30 mL)
Mayonnaise	1 t. (5 mL)
Oil, cooking	1 t. (5 mL)
Gravy	2 T. (30 mL)

Nuts:
Almonds	10 whole
Brazil	2 whole
Cashews	5 whole
Peanuts	12 whole
Pecans	6 halves
Walnuts	6 halves
Olives	5 small
Tartar Sauce	2 t. (10 mL)
Whipped Cream	2 T. (30 mL)

NOTE: If diet requires only polyunsaturated fats, consult your doctor or diet counselor.

Prepared Products

Bread

	Product	Amount	Calories	Exchange
BEST FOODS, CPC INTERNATIONAL	Argo Cornstarch	2 T. (30 mL)	70	1 bread
	Duryea's Cornstarch	2 T. (30 mL)	70	1 bread
	Kingsford Cornstarch	2 T. (30 mL)	70	1 bread
	Presto Self-Rising Cake Flour	2½ T. (35 mL)	60	1 bread
CREAMETTE CO.	Egg Noodles (cooked)	1 c. (250 mL)	220	3 bread
	Macaroni and Cheese Dinner (cooked)	1 c. (250 mL)	240	3 bread 2 fat
	Pasta Misc. (cooked)	1 c. (250 mL)	210	3 bread
GENERAL FOODS	Stove Top Stuffing Mixes	½ c. (125 mL)	180	1½ bread 2 fat
GENERAL MILLS	Bisquick	2 oz. (60 g)	240	2½ bread 1½ fat
	POTATOES: 1 portion, prepared as directed Au Gratin		150	1½ bread 1 fat

Product	Amount	Calories	Exchange
Creamed		160	1½ bread 1 fat
Hash Browns with Onions		150	1½ bread 1 fat
Julienne		130	1 bread 1 fat
Potato Buds		130	1 bread 1 fat
Scalloped		150	1½ bread 1 fat
Sour Cream 'n Chive		140	1 bread 1 fat

PILLSBURY

Product	Amount	Calories	Exchange
PIE CRUSTS: Prepared according to basic recipe			
Mix or Stick	⅛ crust	145	1 bread 1 fat
QUICK BREADS: ½-in. (1.2 cm) slice; 1/16 loaf			
Applesauce Spice		120	1 bread 1 fruit ½ fat
Apricot Nut		110	1 bread ½ fruit ½ fat
Banana		110	1 bread ½ fruit ½ fat
Blueberry Nut		110	1 bread ½ fruit ½ fat
Cherry Nut		130	1 bread 1 fruit 1 fat
Cranberry		120	1 bread 1 fruit ½ fat
Date		120	1 bread 1 fruit ½ fat
Nut		120	1 bread ½ fruit 1 fat
Oatmeal Raisin		120	1 bread 1 fruit ½ fat
OTHER BREADS: Prepared according to basic recipe			
Hot Roll Mix	1 roll	95	1 bread ½ fat
Hotloaf	1 slice	90	1 bread ½ fat
HUNGRY JACK BISCUITS			
Butter Tastin'	2 biscuits	190	1½ bread 2 fat

Product	Amount	Calories	Exchange
Flaky	2 biscuits	180	1½ bread 2 fat
Flaky Buttermilk	2 biscuits	180	1½ bread 2 fat
Fluffy Buttermilk	2 biscuits	190	1½ bread 2 fat

PILLSBURY BISCUITS

Product	Amount	Calories	Exchange
Buttermilk	2 biscuits	110	1½ bread
Country Style	2 biscuits	110	1½ bread
Flaky Tenderflake Buttermilk Dinner	2 biscuits	120	1 bread 1 fat
Tenderflake Baking Powder Dinner	2 biscuits	120	1 bread 1 fat

1869 BRAND BISCUITS

Product	Amount	Calories	Exchange
Baking Powder, Butter Tastin' or Buttermilk	1 biscuit	105	1 bread 1 fat
Heat 'N Eat, Baking Powder or Buttermilk	1 biscuit	100	1 bread 1 fat

HUNGRY JACK POTATOES: Prepared according to basic recipe

Product	Amount	Calories	Exchange
Mashed Potato Flakes	½ c. (125 mL)	140	1 bread 1½ fat

HUNGRY JACK PANCAKE & WAFFLE MIXES: 1 pancake, 4 in. (10 cm) prepared according to basic recipe

Product	Amount	Calories	Exchange
Blueberry		113	1 bread 1 fat
Buttermilk		80	½ bread 1 fat
Complete		73	1 bread
Complete Buttermilk		60	1 bread
Extra Lights		60	½ bread ½ fat

DINNER ROLLS

Product	Amount	Calories	Exchange
Ballard Crescent	2 rolls	190	2 bread 1½ fat
Butterflake	1 roll	100	1 bread ½ fat
Oven Lovin'	2 rolls	110	1 bread ½ fat
Pillsbury Crescent	2 rolls	190	1½ bread 2 fat

MUFFINS

Product	Amount	Calories	Exchange
Apple, Cinnamon, Bran, or Corn	1 muffin	120	1 bread 1 fat

WIENER WRAPS

Product	Amount	Calories	Exchange
Cheese	1 wrap	70	½ bread ½ fat
Plain	1 wrap	60	½ bread ½ fat

Meats

	Product	Amount	Calories	Exchange
FRANCO-AMERICAN	Boned Chicken	2½ oz. (75 g)	110	2 lean meat
	Boned Turkey	2½ oz. (75 g)	110	2 lean meat
	Chicken Spread	1 oz. (30 g)	70	1 lean meat
HORMEL	Coarse-Ground Bologna	2 oz. (60 g)	150	1 high-fat meat ½ vegetable
	Chopped Ham	1 oz. (30 g)	70	1 lean meat ½ fat
	Cooked Ham	2 oz. (60 g)	240	1½ lean meat
	Deviled Ham	1 oz. (30 g)	70	½ lean meat
	Kolbase Polish Sausage	3 oz. (90 g)	70	2 high-fat meat 1 fat
	Meat or Beef Wieners, 1-lb. (500-g) pkg.	1	140	1 high-fat meat 1 fat
	Pepperoni	1 oz. (30 g)	140	1 high-fat meat 1 fat
	Spam	3 oz. (90 g)	260	1½ medium-fat meat ½ vegetable
	Spiced Luncheon Meat	1 oz. (30 g)	80	½ lean meat 1 fat
	Thuringer	1 oz. (30 g)	100	1 high-fat meat
	Tender Chunk Chicken	3 oz. (90 g)	110	2 lean meat
	Tender Chunk Ham	3 oz. (90 g)	140	2 medium-fat meat
	Tender Chunk Turkey	3 oz. (90 g)	90	2 lean meat
OSCAR MAYER	Bar-B-Q Loaf	1 slice	50	½ meat ½ fat
	Beef Bologna	1 slice	75	½ meat 1 fat
	Beef Cotto Salami	1 slice	50	½ meat ½ fat
	Beef Franks	1	140	½ meat 2 fat
	Braunschweiger	1 slice	70	½ meat 1 fat

Product	Amount	Calories	Exchange
Beef Summer Sausage	1 oz. (30 g)	100	½ meat 1½ fat
Chopped Ham	1 slice	65	½ meat ½ fat
Cooked Ham	1 slice	30	½ meat
Hard Salami	1 slice	35	¼ meat ½ fat
Honey Loaf	1 slice	35	½ meat
Jubilee Canned Ham	1 oz. (30 g)	35	½ meat
Little Friers Pork Sausage	1	65	½ meat 1 fat
New England Brand Sausage	1	35	½ meat
Sandwich Spread	1 oz. (30 g)	60	½ meat ½ fat

Casseroles and One-Dish Meals

	Product	Amount	Calories	Exchange
FRANCO-AMERICAN	Beef Ravioli in Meat Sauce	7½ oz. (225 g)	220	1 vegetable 2 bread 1 lean meat
	Elbow Macaroni & Cheese	7¼ oz. (220 g)	180	2 bread 1 fat
	Rotini in Tomato Sauce	7½ oz. (225 g)	200	1 vegetable 1 fat
	Spaghetti in Meat Sauce	7¾ oz. (230 g)	220	1 vegetable 1 bread 1 lean meat 1 fat
	Spaghetti-O's in Tomato & Cheese Sauce	7½ oz. (225 g)	160	2 bread
GENERAL MILLS	MUG 'O LUNCH: 1 pouch			
	Macaroni & Cheese Sauce		230	2 bread ½ milk 1 fat
	Noodles & Beef-Flavored Sauce		170	2 bread ½ fat
	Noodles & Chicken-Flavored Sauce		150	2 bread ½ fat
	Oriental Noodles & Sauces		190	2 bread ½ fat
	Spaghetti & Tomato Sauce		160	2½ bread
	HAMBURGER HELPER: 1 portion, prepared as directed			
	Beef Noodle		320	2 bread 2 medium-fat meat ½ fat

Product	Amount	Calories	Exchange
Cheeseburger Macaroni		360	1½ bread ½ milk 2 medium-fat meat 1 fat
Chili Tomato		320	1½ bread 1 vegetable 2 medium-fat meat ½ fat
Lasagne		330	2 bread 2 medium-fat meat ½ fat
Hamburger Pizza Dish		340	2 bread 2 medium-fat meat ½ fat
Hamburger Stew		290	1 bread 1 vegetable 2 medium-fat meat 1 fat
Hash Dinner		300	1½ bread 2 medium-fat meat 1 fat
Potato Stroganoff		330	2 bread 2 medium-fat meat ½ fat
Rice Oriental	8-oz. pkg. (240-g pkg.)	340	2 bread 2 medium-fat meat ½ fat
Rice Oriental	6½-oz. pkg. (195-g pkg.)	300	1½ bread 2 medium-fat meat ½ fat
Spaghetti		330	2 bread 2 medium-fat meat ½ fat
TUNA HELPER: 1 portion, prepared as directed			
Country Dumplings 'n Tuna		230	2 bread 1 lean meat ½ fat
Creamy Noodles 'n Tuna		280	2 bread 1 lean meat 1½ fat
Noodles, Cheese Sauce 'n Tuna		230	1½ bread ½ milk 1 lean meat ½ fat

	Product	Amount	Calories	Exchange
	CASSEROLES AND SIDE DISHES: 1 portion, prepared as directed			
	Macaroni and Cheese		310	2 bread ½ milk 3 fat
	Noodles Almondine		240	1½ bread ¼ milk 2½ fat
	Noodles Romanoff		230	1 bread ½ milk 2½ fat
	Noodles Stroganoff		230	1½ bread ½ milk 2 fat
HORMEL	SHORT ORDERS: 7½-oz. (225-g) can			
	Beans 'n Wieners		290	1 high-fat meat 1 fat 2 bread
	Beef Goulash		230	2 medium-fat meat 1 bread
	Chili with Beans		300	2 high-fat meat 1½ bread
	Chili Mac		200	1 high-fat meat ½ fat 1 bread
	Lasagne		260	1 high-fat meat 1½ fat 1½ bread
	Noodles 'n Beef		230	1½ medium-fat meat 1 fat 1 bread
	Pork Chow Mein		140	½ lean meat 1 fat 2½ vegetable
	Scalloped Potatoes 'n Ham		250	1 medium-fat meat 2 fat 1 bread ½ vegetable
	Spaghetti 'n Beef		240	1 high-fat meat 1 fat 1½ bread

	Product	Amount	Calories	Exchange
SWANSON	**FROZEN MEAT PIES:** 1 complete pie			
	Beef	8 oz. (240 g)	430	3 bread 1 lean meat 4 fat
	Chicken and Turkey	8 oz. (240 g)	450	3 bread 1 lean meat 4 fat
	Macaroni and Cheese	7 oz. (210 g)	230	2 bread 1 lean meat 1 fat
	HUNGRY MAN MEAT PIES:			
	Beef	16 oz. (480 g)	770	1 vegetable 4 bread 3 lean meat 7 fat
	Chicken	16 oz. (480 g)	780	1 vegetable 4 bread 3 lean meat 7 fat
	Sirloin Burger	16 oz. (480 g)	800	1 vegetable 4 bread 3 lean meat 7 fat
	Turkey	16 oz. (480 g)	790	1 vegetable 4 bread 3 lean meat 7 fat
	ENTREES: 1 complete entree			
	Chicken Nibbles with French Fries	6 oz. (180 g)	370	2 bread 2 lean meat 3 fat
	Fried Chicken with Whipped Potatoes	7 oz. (210 g)	360	2 bread 2 lean meat 2 fat
	Gravy & Sliced Beef with Whipped Potatoes	8 oz. (240 g)	190	1½ bread 1 lean meat 1 fat
	Salisbury Steak with Crinkle-Cut Potatoes	5½ oz. (195 g)	370	2 bread 2 lean meat 3 fat
	Spaghetti with Breaded Veal	8¼ oz. (250 g)	290	2 bread 1 lean meat 2 fat
	Turkey/Gravy/Dressing with Whipped Potatoes	8¾ oz. (280 g)	260	2 bread 2 lean meat
	HUNGRY MAN ENTREES:			
	Barbecue Chicken with Whipped Potatoes	12 oz. (360 g)	550	3 bread 4 lean meat 3 fat
	Lasagne and Garlic Roll	12¾ oz. (385 g)	540	3 bread 2 lean meat 5 fat

175

Product	Amount	Calories	Exchange
Sliced Beef with Whipped Potatoes	12¼ oz. (370 g)	330	1½ bread 4 lean meat
Turkey/Gravy/Dressing with Whipped Potatoes	13¼ oz. (400 g)	380	2 bread 4 lean meat

Sandwiches and Snacks

	Product	Amount	Calories	Exchange
BEST FOODS, CPC INTERNATIONAL	Skippy Dry-Roasted Peanuts, Cashews, Mixed Nuts	1 oz. (30 g)	165	1 medium-fat meat 2 fat
GENERAL MILLS	Beef Jerky	1 strip	25	½ lean meat
KRAFT PIZZA	Cheese	¼ pizza	250	2½ bread 1 medium-fat meat
	Sausage	¼ pizza	280	2½ bread 1 fat 1 medium-fat meat
ORE-IDA FOODS	Onion Ringers	2 oz. (60 g)	160	1 bread 2 fat
	La Pizzeria Pizza, Combination Sausage	6.8 oz. (200 g)	420	3 bread 2 fat 2 medium-fat meat
	La Pizzeria Pizza, Pepperoni	5.3 oz. (160 g)	330	3 bread 1 fat 2 medium-fat meat
	La Pizzeria Pizza, Thick Crust, Cheese	6.2 oz. (180 g)	410	3 bread 1 fat 2 medium-fat meat
PLANTERS	OIL-ROASTED NUTS: Cashews	1 oz. (30 g)	180	1 bread 1 high-fat meat
	Mixed (with peanuts)	1 oz. (30 g)	185	1 fruit or ½ bread 1 high-fat meat
	Mixed (without peanuts)	1 oz. (30 g)	180	1 fruit or ½ bread 1 high-fat meat
	Peanuts	¾ oz. (22 g)	130	1 high-fat meat

Product	Amount	Calories	Exchange
Spanish Peanuts	1 oz. (30 g)	180	1½ high-fat meat
DRY-ROASTED NUTS: Almonds	1 oz. (30 g)	185	1 fruit or ½ bread 1 high-fat meat
Cashews	1 oz. (30 g)	180	1 bread or 1 fruit 1 high-fat meat
Mixed	1 oz. (30 g)	175	1 fruit or ½ bread 1 high-fat meat
Peanuts	1 oz. (30 g)	170	1 fruit or ½ bread 1 high-fat meat
Pecans	1 oz. (30 g)	205	½ high-fat meat 2 fat
Spanish Peanuts	1 oz. (30 g)	175	1½ high-fat meat

	Fast-Food Items	Amount	Calories	Exchange
BURGER CHEF	Hamburger	1	250	1½ bread 1 meat 1½ fat
	Double Hamburger	1	325	2 bread 2½ meat 1 fat
	Super Chef	1	530	2½ bread 3½ meat 2 fat
	Big Chef	1	535	3 bread 3 meat 3 fat
	French Fries	1	240	2 bread 2 fat
	Chocolate Milk Shake	1	310	3 bread ½ meat 1 fat
BURGER KING	Hamburger	1	240	1½ bread 1 medium-fat meat 1 fat
	Double Meat Hamburger	1	370	1½ bread 3 medium-fat meat 1 fat
	Cheeseburger	1	310	2 bread 2 medium-fat meat 1 fat

177

Fast-Food Items	Amount	Calories	Exchange
Double Meat Cheeseburger	1	420	2 bread 3 medium- fat meat 1½ fat
Whopper, Jr.	1	300	2 bread 1 medium- fat meat 2 fat
Whopper, Jr. with Cheese	1	350	2 bread 2 medium- fat meat 2 fat
Double Meat Whopper, Jr.	1	410	2 bread 2 medium- fat meat 3 fat
Double Meat Whopper, Jr. with Cheese	1	460	2 bread 3 medium- fat meat 2½ fat
Whopper	1	650	3½ bread 3 medium- fat meat 4½ fat
Whopper with Cheese	1	760	3½ bread 4 medium- fat meat 5½ fat
Double Meat Whopper	1	870	3½ bread 5 medium- fat meat 6 fat
Double Meat Whopper with Cheese	1	980	3½ bread 6 medium- fat meat 6½ fat
Whaler	1	720	4½ bread 4 lean meat 4½ fat
Whaler with Cheese	1	820	4½ bread 5 lean meat 6 fat
Yumbo	1	410	2 bread 3 medium- fat meat 1 fat
Hot Dog	1	290	1½ bread 1 high-fat meat 2 fat
French Fries (small)	1	200	2 bread 2 fat
French Fries (large)	1	320	3 bread 3 fat
Onion Rings (small)	1	150	1 bread 1 vegetable 1½ fat

	Fast-Food Items	Amount	Calories	Exchange
	Onion Rings (large)	1	220	2 bread
				1 vegetable
				2 fat
	Diet Dr. Pepper, Diet 7-Up, or Diet Tab	12 oz. (360 g)	2	free
KENTUCKY FRIED CHICKEN				
	Fried chicken, mashed potato, coleslaw, rolls			
	Original 3-piece dinner		830	4 bread
				6 meat
				2½ fat
	Crispy 3-piece dinner		1070	5 bread
				6 meat
				6½ fat
	Original 2-piece dinner		595	3½ bread
				2 meat
				1½ fat
	Crispy 2-piece dinner		665	3 bread
				4½ meat
				3½ fat
MCDONALDS	Hamburger	1	260	1½ bread
				1 meat
				1½ fat
	Double Hamburger	1	350	2 bread
				2 meat
				1 fat
	Quarter Pounder	1	420	2½ bread
				3 meat
				1 fat
	Big Mac	1	550	3 bread
				2 meat
				4 fat
	French Fries	1	180	1½ bread
				2 fat
	Chocolate Milk Shake	1	315	3½ bread
				1½ fat
PIZZA HUT	Cheese pizza			
	Thick Crust, individual	1	1030	9½ bread
				7½ meat
	Thin Crust, individual	1	1005	8½ bread
				6 meat
	Thick Crust, 13 in. (32.5 cm)	half	900	7½ bread
				7 meat
	Thin Crust, 13 in. (32.5 cm)	half	850	7 bread
				5 meat
	Thick Crust, 15 in. (37.5 cm)	half	1200	10 bread
				9 meat
	Thin Crust, 15 in. (37.5 cm)	half	1150	9½ bread
				7 meat

	Fast-Food Items	Amount	Calories	Exchange
TOTINO'S	PARTY PIZZAS:			
	Cheese, 13 oz. (369 g)	half	440	3 bread 1 vegetable 2 medium- fat meat 1 fat
	Hamburger, 13½ oz. (383 g)	half	460	3 bread 1 vegetable 2 medium- fat meat 2 fat
	Pepperoni, 13 oz. (369 g)	half	460	3 bread 1 vegetable 2 medium- fat meat 1½ fat
	Sausage, 13½ oz. (383 g)	half	470	3 bread 1 vegetable 2 medium- fat meat 1½ fat
	CLASSIC PIZZAS:			
	Classic Combination, 22½ oz. (638 g)	one-third	520	3 bread 1 vegetable 2 medium- fat meat 3 fat
	Classic Sausage, 21½ oz. (609 g)	one-third	500	3 bread 1 vegetable 2 medium- fat meat 2½ fat

Sauces and Salad Dressings

	Product	Amount	Calories	Exchange
BEST FOODS, CPC INTERNATIONAL	Hellman's French	1 T. (15 mL)	60	1 fat
	Hellman's Real Mayonnaise	1 t. (5 mL)	35	1 fat
	Hellman's Sandwich Spread	2 t. (10 mL)	40	1 fat
	Hellman's Spin Blend	2 t. (10 mL)	40	1 fat
	Hellman's Tartar Sauce	2 t. (10 mL)	50	1 fat
CAMPBELL'S	Beef Gravy	2 oz. (60 g)	30	1 fat
	Brown Gravy with Onions	2 oz. (60 g)	25	1 fat
	Chicken Gravy	2 oz. (60 g)	50	1 fat

	Product	Amount	Calories	Exchange
	Chicken Giblet Gravy	2 oz. (60 g)	35	1 fat
	Mushroom Gravy	2 oz. (60 g)	35	1 fat
CHIFFON PRODUCTS	Lo-Cal French	1 T. (15 mL)	25	½ fat
	Lo-Cal Italian	1 T. (15 mL)	40	1 fat
	Seven Seas Salad Dressing	1 T. (15 mL)	70	1½ fat
R. T. FRENCH CO.	Au Jus Gravy	¼ c. (60 mL)	8	free
	Brown Gravy	¼ c. (60 mL)	20	free
	Cheese Sauce	¼ c. (60 mL)	80	½ milk 1 fat
	Hollandaise Sauce	3 T. (45 mL)	45	1 fat
	Sour Cream Sauce	2½ T. (32 mL)	60	½ milk 1 fat
KRAFT DRESSINGS	Lo-Cal Bleu Cheese	1 T. (15 mL)	14	free
	Lo-Cal Catalina	1 T. (15 mL)	16	free
	Lo-Cal Coleslaw	1 T. (15 mL)	30	½ fat
	Lo-Cal French	1 T. (15 mL)	25	½ fat
	Lo-Cal Italian	1 T. (15 mL)	8	free
	Miracle Whip	1 T. (15 mL)	70	1½ fat
	Real Mayonnaise	1 T. (15 mL)	100	2 fat
PILLSBURY	Brown or Home Style Gravy	½ c. (125 mL)	30	½ bread
	Chicken Gravy	½ c. (125 mL)	30	½ bread
RAGU FOODS, INC.	Plain Spaghetti Sauce	5 oz. (150 g)	110	1 bread 1 fat
	Thick and Zesty Plain Spaghetti Sauce	5 oz. (150 g)	130	1 bread 1 fat
WESTERN DRESSING, INC.	Barbecue Sauce	1 T. (15 mL)	24	½ fruit
	Chunky Bleu Cheese	1 T. (15 mL)	75	1 fat
	Regular Mayonnaise	1 T. (15 mL)	96	2 fat

Soups and Stews

	Product	Amount	Calories	Exchange
CAMPBELL'S	CONDENSED SOUPS: Prepared			
	Asparagus, Cream of	10 oz. (300 g)	100	1 bread 1 fat
	Bean with Bacon	11 oz. (330 g)	200	2 bread 1 lean meat ½ fat
	Beef	11 oz. (330 g)	110	1 bread 1 lean meat
	Beef Noodle	10 oz. (300 g)	90	1 bread
	Black Bean	11 oz. (330 g)	150	1½ bread
	Celery, Cream of	10 oz. (300 g)	110	½ bread 1½ fat
	Chicken Alphabet	10 oz. (300 g)	110	1 bread 1 fat
	Chicken, Cream of	10 oz. (300 g)	140	½ bread 2 fat
	Chicken 'n Dumplings	10 oz. (300 g)	120	½ bread 1 lean meat 1 fat
	Chicken Noodle	10 oz. (300 g)	90	1 bread
	Chicken Noodle O's	10 oz. (300 g)	90	1 bread
	Clam Chowder (Manhattan Style)	10 oz. (300 g)	100	1 bread ½ fat
	Mushroom, Cream of	10 oz. (300 g)	150	1 bread 2 fat
	Mushroom, Golden	10 oz. (300 g)	110	1 bread 1 fat
	Noodles & Ground Beef	10 oz. (300 g)	110	1 bread 1 fat
	Stockpot	11 oz. (330 g)	130	1 bread 1 lean meat
	Tomato	10 oz. (300 g)	110	1 vegetable 1 bread
	Tomato-Beef Noodle O's	10 oz. (300 g)	160	1½ bread 1 fat
	Turkey Noodle	10 oz. (300 g)	80	1 bread
	Turkey Vegetable	10 oz. (300 g)	90	1 bread
	Vegetarian Vegetable	10 oz. (300 g)	90	1 bread
	SOUPS FOR ONE: 11⅝-oz. (350-g) can, undiluted Bean, Old Fashioned		210	2 bread 1 fat

Product	Amount	Calories	Exchange
Clam Chowder, New England (made with milk)		200	½ milk 1 bread 1 lean meat
Golden Chicken & Noodles		120	1 bread 1 fat
Tomato Royale		180	2 bread 1 fat
Vegetable, Old World		125	1 bread 1 fat
CHUNKY SOUPS: half of a 19-oz. (539-g) can, undiluted			
Chunky Beef		190	1 bread 2 lean meat
Chunky Chicken		200	1 vegetable 1 bread 2 lean meat
Chunky Chili Beef		260	2 bread 2 lean meat
Chunky Old Fashioned Vegetable Beef		160	1 vegetable 1 bread 1 lean meat
Chunky Sirloin Burger		210	1 vegetable 1 bread 1 lean meat 1 fat
Chunky Steak & Potato		190	1 bread 2 lean meat
Chunky Vegetable		140	1 vegetable 1 bread 1 fat
DINTY MOORE Beef Stew	7½ oz. (225 g)	180	1½ medium-fat meat 1 bread
Vegetable Stew	7½ oz. (225 g)	160	1½ high-fat meat 1 bread ½ fat

Alcohol

Amount	Type	Calories	Carbohydrates (grams)	Exchange
12 oz.	Beer	170	16	1 bread 2 fat
1½ oz.	Gin, Rum, Whiskey, Vodka	120	0	3 fat
3½ oz.	Dry Wine	85	4	⅓ bread 1½ fat
2 oz.	Dry Sherry	85	5	⅓ bread 1½ fat

(Carbohydrate in these beverages is indicated by bread exchanges; alcohol is indicated by fat exchanges.)

The Six Major Exchange Lists *

The updated **Exchange Lists For Meal Planning** reflect the most current thinking in the area of nutrition education. Based on concern for total caloric intake and for modifications of fat intake the Exchange Lists now include many revisions and additions.

LIST 1, Milk Exchanges, now includes Non-Fat, Low-Fat and Whole Milk. **LIST 2,** Vegetable Exchanges, includes all vegetables except Starchy Vegetables. Vegetables on **LIST 2** average 25 calories for one-half cup servings. Starchy Vegetables appear in **LIST 4,** Bread Exchanges. **LIST 5,** Meat Exchanges, includes not only Lean Meat, but also Medium-Fat and High-Fat Meats and other protein-rich foods. **LIST 6,** Fat Exchanges, has been revised to show differences in the kind of fat contained in them—Saturated or Poly-unsaturated. Saturated fat has been associated with an *increase* in blood cholesterol (a possible risk factor in coronary heart disease). The physician may advise a reduction of foods high in this kind of fat. Polyunsaturated fat has been associated with a *decrease* in blood cholesterol. You then may advise substituting foods containing this kind of fat whenever possible. **Bold type** is used in this booklet to indicate Low-Fat foods or foods high in polyunsaturated fats.

If variety is the spice of life, Exchange Lists are just what you're looking for.

What do we mean by Exchange Lists? When we think of an "exchange" we automatically think of a "substitute" or a "trade." (I'll trade you an apple for an orange.) Basically, that's how it works, but the possibilities are endless.

Diets are sometimes stated in very dull, specific terms. For example:

Orange juice	1/2 cup
Oatmeal	1/2 cup
Rye toast	1 slice
Soft cooked egg	1
Butter	1 teaspoon
Milk	1/2 pint

Exchange Lists take the dreariness out of diets. The Lists are groups of measured foods of the same value that can be substituted in Meal Plans. Foods have been divided into six groups, or Exchanges. For example, vegetables are listed in one group and fats are listed in another group. Foods in any *one group* can be substituted or exchanged with other foods in the *same group.*

Within each group an Exchange is approximately equal in calories and in the amount of carbohydrate, protein and fat. In addition, each Exchange contains similar minerals and vitamins.

The number of calories in any food expresses the energy value of the food. As an adult you may need fewer calories to maintain normal weight. Many people as they reach their 30's and 40's become physically less active but do not change their eating habits. They store their excess calories as fat. The result: the famous "middle age spread." Your diet counselor will know how many calories you require each day to maintain good health.

Fats, carbohydrates and proteins are the three major energy sources in foods. The most common carbohydrates are sugars and starches. Proteins yield energy and contain nitrogen, which is essential for life. Fats provide energy and are the most concentrated source of calories. Alcohol also contributes calories.

Minerals and vitamins are substances present in food in small amounts and perform essential functions in the body. The foods of each Exchange make a specific nutritional contribution. No one Exchange group can supply all the nutrients needed for a well-balanced diet. It takes all six of them working together as a team to supply your nutritional needs for good health.

* The exchange lists are based on material in *Exchange Lists for Meal Planning* prepared by Committees of the American Diabetes Association, Inc., and the American Dietetic Association in cooperation with the National Institute of Arthritis, Metabolism and Digestive Diseases and the National Heart and Lung Institute, National Institutes of Health, Public Health Service, U.S. Department of Health, Education and Welfare.

LIST 1

Milk Exchanges
(Includes **Non-Fat** Low-Fat and Whole Milk)

One Exchange of Milk contains 12 grams of carbohydrate, 8 grams of protein, a trace of fat and 80 calories.

Milk is a basic food for your Meal Plan for very good reasons. Milk is the leading source of calcium. It is a good source of phosphorus, protein, some of the B-complex vitamins, including folacin and vitamin B_{12}, and vitamins A and D. Magnesium is also found in milk. ,

Since it is a basic ingredient in many recipes you will not find it difficult to include milk in your Meal Plan. Milk can be used not only to drink but can be added to cereal, coffee, tea and other foods.

This List shows the kinds and amounts of milk or milk products to use for one Milk Exchange. Those which appear in **bold type** are **non-fat**. Low-Fat and Whole Milk contain saturated fat.

Non-Fat Fortified Milk

Skim or non-fat milk	1 cup
Powdered (non-fat dry, before adding liquid)	1/3 cup
Canned, evaporated — skim milk	1/2 cup
Buttermilk made from skim milk	1 cup
Yogurt made from skim milk (plain, unflavored)	1 cup

Low-Fat Fortified Milk

1% fat fortified milk (omit 1/2 Fat Exchange)	1 cup
2% fat fortified milk (omit 1 Fat Exchange)	1 cup
Yogurt made from 2% fortified milk (plain, unflavored) (omit 1 Fat Exchange)	1 cup

Whole Milk (Omit 2 Fat Exchanges)

Whole milk	1 cup
Canned, evaporated whole milk	1/2 cup
Buttermilk made from whole milk	1 cup
Yogurt made from whole milk (plain, unflavored)	1 cup

LIST 2  Vegetable Exchanges

One Exchange of Vegetables contains about 5 grams of carbohydrate, 2 grams of protein and 25 calories.

The generous use of many vegetables, served either alone or in other foods such as casseroles, soups or salads, contributes to sound health and vitality.

Dark green and deep yellow vegetables are among the leading sources of vitamin A. Many of the vegetables in this group are notable sources of vitamin C — asparagus, broccoli, brussels sprouts, cabbage, cauliflower, collards, kale, dandelion, mustard and turnip greens, spinach, rutabagas, to tomatoes and turnips. A number, including broccoli, brussels sprouts, beet greens, chard and tomato juice, are particularly good sources of potassium. High folacin values are found in asparagus, beets, broccoli, brussels sprouts, cauliflower, collards, kale and lettuce. Moderate amounts of vitamin B_6 are supplied by broccoli, brussels sprouts, cauliflower, collards, spinach, sauerkraut and tomatoes and tomato juice. Fiber is present in all vegetables.

Whether you serve them cooked or raw, wash all vegetables even though they look clean. If fat is added in the preparation, omit the equivalent number of Fat Exchanges. The average amount of fat contained in a Vegetable Exchange that is cooked with fat meat or other fats is one Fat Exchange.

This List shows the kinds of **vegetables** to use for one Vegetable Exchange. One Exchange is ½ cup.

Asparagus	Greens:
Bean Sprouts	Mustard
Beets	Spinach
Broccoli	Turnip
Brussels Sprouts	Mushrooms
Cabbage	Okra
Carrots	Onions
Cauliflower	Rhubarb
Celery	Rutabaga
Eggplant	Sauerkraut
Green Pepper	String Beans, green or yellow
Greens:	Summer Squash
Beet	Tomatoes
Chards	Tomato Juice
Collards	Turnips
Dandelion	Vegetable Juice Cocktail
Kale	Zucchini

The following **raw vegetables** may be used as desired:

Chicory	Lettuce
Chinese Cabbage	Parsley
Cucumbers	Pickles, Dill
Endive	Radishes
Escarole	Watercress

Starchy Vegetables are found in the Bread Exchange List.

LIST  **Fruit Exchanges**

One Exchange of Fruit contains 10 grams of carbohydrate and 40 calories.

Everyone likes to buy fresh fruits when they are in the height of their season. But you can also buy fresh fruits and can or freeze them for off-season use. For variety serve fruit as a salad or in combination with other foods for dessert.

Fruits are valuable for vitamins, minerals and fiber. Vitamin C is abundant in citrus fruits and fruit juices and is found in raspberries, strawberries, mangoes, cantaloupes, honeydews and papayas. The better sources of vitamin A among these fruits include fresh or dried apricots, mangoes, cantaloupes, nectarines, yellow peaches and persimmons. Oranges, orange juice and cantaloupe provide more folacin than most of the other fruits in this listing. Many fruits are a valuable source of potassium, especially apricots, bananas, several of the berries, grapefruit, grapefruit juice, mangoes, cantaloupes, honeydews, nectarines, oranges, orange juice and peaches.

Fruit may be used fresh, dried, canned or frozen, cooked or raw, as long as no sugar is added.

This List shows the kinds and amounts of **fruits** to use for one Fruit Exchange.

Apple	1 small	**Apricots, fresh**	2 medium
Apple Juice	1/3 cup	**Apricots, dried**	4 halves
Applesauce (unsweetened)	1/2 cup	**Banana**	1/2 small

Berries			Honeydew	1/8 medium
Blackberries	1/2 cup		Watermelon	1 cup
Blueberries	1/2 cup		Nectarine	1 small
Raspberries	1/2 cup		Orange	1 small
Strawberries	3/4 cup		Orange Juice	1/2 cup
Cherries	10 large		Papaya	3/4 cup
Cider	1/3 cup		Peach	1 medium
Dates	2		Pear	1 small
Figs, fresh	1		Persimmon, native	1 medium
Figs, dried	1		Pineapple	1/2 cup
Grapefruit	1/2		Pineapple Juice	1/3 cup
Grapefruit Juice	1/2 cup		Plums	2 medium
Grapes	12		Prunes	2 medium
Grape Juice	1/4 cup		Prune Juice	1/4 cup
Mango	1/2 small		Raisins	2 tablespoons
Melon			Tangerine	1 medium
Cantaloupe	1/4 small			

Cranberries may be used as desired if no sugar is added.

LIST 4

Bread Exchanges
(Includes **Bread, Cereal** and **Starchy Vegetables**)

One Exchange of Bread contains 15 grams of carbohydrate, 2 grams of protein and 70 calories.

In this List, whole-grain and enriched breads and cereals, germ and bran products and dried beans and peas are good sources of iron and among the better sources of thiamin. The whole-grain, bran and germ products have more fiber than products made from refined flours. Dried beans and peas are also good sources of fiber. Wheat germ, bran, dried beans, potatoes, lima beans, parsnips, pumpkin and winter squash are particularly good sources of potassium. The better sources of folacin in this listing include whole-wheat bread, wheat germ, dried beans, corn, lima beans, parsnips, green peas, pumpkin and sweet potato.

Starchy vegetables are included in this List, because they contain the same amount of carbohydrate and protein as one slice of bread.

This List shows the kinds and amounts of **Breads, Cereals, Starchy Vegetables** and Prepared Foods to use for one Bread Exchange. Those which appear in **bold type** are **low-fat.**

Bread

White (including French and Italian)	1 slice
Whole Wheat	1 slice
Rye or Pumpernickel	1 slice
Raisin	1 slice
Bagel, small	1/2
English Muffin, small	1/2
Plain Roll, bread	1
Frankfurter Roll	1/2
Hamburger Bun	1/2
Dried Bread Crumbs	3 Tbs.
Tortilla, 6"	1

Cereal

Bran Flakes	1/2 cup
Other ready-to-eat unsweetened Cereal	3/4 cup
Puffed Cereal (unfrosted)	1 cup
Cereal (cooked)	1/2 cup
Grits (cooked)	1/2 cup
Rice or Barley (cooked)	1/2 cup
Pasta (cooked), Spaghetti, Noodles, Macaroni	1/2 cup
Popcorn (popped, no fat added, large kernel)	3 cups
Cornmeal (dry)	2 Tbs.
Flour	2-1/2 Tbs.
Wheat Germ	1/4 cup

Crackers

Arrowroot	3
Graham, 2-1/2" sq.	2
Matzoth, 4" x 6"	1/2
Oyster	20

Pretzels, 3-1/8" long x 1/8" dia.	25	Prepared Foods	
Rye Wafers, 2" x 3-1/2"	3	Biscuit 2" dia. (omit 1 Fat Exchange)	1
Saltines	6	Corn Bread, 2"x 2"x 1" (omit 1 Fat Exchange)	1
Soda, 2-1/2" sq.	4	Corn Muffin, 2" dia. (omit 1 Fat Exchange)	1
Dried Beans, Peas and Lentils		Crackers, round butter type (omit 1 Fat Exchange)	5
Beans, Peas, Lentils (dried and cooked)	1/2 cup	Muffin, plain small (omit 1 Fat Exchange)	1
Baked Beans, no pork (canned)	1/4 cup	Potatoes, French Fried, length 2" to 3-1/2" (omit 1 Fat Exchange)	8
Starchy Vegetables		Potato or Corn Chips (omit 2 Fat Exchanges)	15
Corn	1/3 cup	Pancake, 5" x 1/2" (omit 1 Fat Exchange)	1
Corn on Cob	1 small	Waffle, 5" x 1/2" (omit 1 Fat Exchange)	1
Lima Beans	1/2 cup		
Parsnips	2/3 cup		
Peas, Green (canned or frozen)	1/2 cup		
Potato, White	1 small		
Potato (mashed)	1/2 cup		
Pumpkin	3/4 cup		
Winter Squash, Acorn or Butternut	1/2 cup		
Yam or Sweet Potato	1/4 cup		

LIST 5   Meat Exchanges Lean Meat

One Exchange of Lean Meat (1 oz.) contains 7 grams of protein, 3 grams of fat and 55 calories.

All of the foods in the Meat Exchange Lists are good sources of protein and many are also good sources of iron, zinc, vitamin B_{12} (present only in foods of animal origin) and other vitamins of the vitamin B-complex.

Cholesterol is of animal origin. Foods of plant origin have no cholesterol.

Oysters are outstanding for their high content of zinc. Crab, liver, trimmed lean meats, the dark muscle meat of turkey, dried beans and peas and peanut butter all have much less zinc than oysters but are still good sources.

Dried beans, peas and peanut butter are particularly good sources of magnesium; also potassium.

Your choice of meat groups through the week will depend on your blood lipid values. Consult with your diet counselor and your physician regarding your selection.

You may use the meat, fish or other Meat Exchanges that are prepared for the family when no fat or flour has been added. If meat is fried, use the fat included in the Meal Plan. Meat juices with the fat removed may be used with your meat or vegetables for added flavor. **Be certain to trim off all visible fat** and measure after it has been cooked. A three-ounce serving of cooked meat is about equal to four ounces of raw meat.

To plan a diet low in saturated fat and cholesterol, choose only those Exchanges in **bold type**.

This List shows the kinds and amounts of **Lean Meat** and other Protein-Rich Foods to use for one Low-Fat Meat Exchange. **Trim off all visible fat.**

Beef:	**Baby Beef (very lean), Chipped Beef, Chuck, Flank Steak, Tenderloin, Plate Ribs, Plate Skirt Steak, Round (bottom, top), All cuts Rump, Spare Ribs, Tripe**	1 oz.
Lamb:	**Leg, Rib, Sirloin, Loin (roast and chops), Shank, Shoulder**	1 oz.
Pork:	**Leg (Whole Rump, Center Shank), Ham, Smoked (center slices)**	1 oz.
Veal:	**Leg, Loin, Rib, Shank, Shoulder, Cutlets**	1 oz.

Poultry: Meat <u>without skin</u> **of Chicken, Turkey, Cornish Hen,**
         Guinea Hen, Pheasant   1 oz.

Fish: **Any fresh or frozen**   1 oz.

        Canned Salmon, Tuna, Mackerel, Crab and Lobster,   1/4 cup

        Clams, Oysters, Scallops, Shrimp,   5 or 1 oz.

        Sardines, drained   3

Cheeses containing less than 5% butterfat   1 oz.

Cottage Cheese, Dry and 2% butterfat   1/4 cup

Dried Beans and Peas (omit 1 Bread Exchange)   1/2 cup

LIST   **Meat Exchanges**
Medium-Fat Meat

One Exhange of Medium-Fat Meat (1 oz.) contains 7 grams of protein, 5 grams of fat and 75 calories.

This List shows the kinds and amounts of Medium-Fat Meat and other Protein-Rich Foods to use for one Medium-Fat Meat Exchange. **Trim off all visible fat.**

Beef:	Ground (15% fat), Corned Beef (canned), Rib Eye, Round (ground commercial)	1 oz.
Pork:	Loin (all cuts Tenderloin), Shoulder Arm (picnic), Shoulder Blade, Boston Butt, Canadian Bacon, Boiled Ham	1 oz.
	Liver, Heart, Kidney and Sweetbreads (these are high in cholesterol)	1 oz.
	Cottage Cheese, creamed	1/4 cup
	Cheese: Mozzarella, Ricotta, Farmer's cheese, Neufchatel, Parmesan	1 oz.
		3 tbs.
	Egg (high in cholesterol)	1
	Peanut Butter (omit 2 additional Fat Exchanges)	2 tbs.

LIST   **Meat Exchanges**
High-Fat Meat

One Exchange of High-Fat Meat (1 oz.) contains 7 grams of protein, 8 grams of fat and 100 calories.

This List shows the kinds and amounts of High-Fat Meat and other Protein-Rich Foods to use for one High-Fat Meat Exchange. **Trim off all visible fat.**

Beef:	Brisket, Corned Beef (Brisket), Ground Beef (more than 20% fat), Hamburger (commercial), Chuck (ground commercial), Roasts (Rib), Steaks (Club and Rib)	1 oz.
Lamb:	Breast	1 oz.
Pork:	Spare Ribs, Loin (Back Ribs), Pork (ground), Country style Ham, Deviled Ham	1 oz.
Veal:	Breast	1 oz.
Poultry:	Capon, Duck (domestic), Goose	1 oz.
Cheese:	Cheddar Types	1 oz.
Cold Cuts		4-1/2"x 1/8" slice
Frankfurter		1 small

LIST 6   **Fat Exchanges**

One Exchange of Fat contains
5 grams of fat and 45 calories.

Fats are of both animal and vegetable origin and range from liquid oils to hard fats.

Oils are fats that remain liquid at room temperature and are usually of vegetable origin. Common fats obtained from vegetables are corn oil, olive oil and peanut oil. Some of the common animal fats are butter and bacon fat.

Since all fats are concentrated sources of calories, foods on this List should be measured carefully to control weight. Margarine, butter, cream and cream cheese contain vitamin A. Use the fats on this List in the amounts on the Meal Plan.

This List shows the kinds and amounts of Fat-Containing Foods to use for one Fat Exchange. To plan a diet low in Saturated Fat select only those Exchanges which appear in **bold type**. They are **Polyunsaturated.**

Margarine, soft, tub or stick*	1 teaspoon
Avocado (4″ in diameter)**	1/8
Oil, Corn, Cottonseed, Safflower,	
Soy, Sunflower	1 teaspoon
Oil, Olive**	1 teaspoon
Oil, Peanut**	1 teaspoon
Olives**	5 small
Almonds**	10 whole
Pecans**	2 large whole
Peanuts**	
Spanish	20 whole
Virginia	10 whole
Walnuts	6 small
Nuts, other**	6 small
Margarine, regular stick	1 teaspoon
Butter	1 teaspoon
Bacon fat	1 teaspoon
Bacon, crisp	1 strip
Cream, light	2 tablespoons
Cream, sour	2 tablespoons
Cream, heavy	1 tablespoon
Cream Cheese	1 tablespoon
French dressing***	1 tablespoon
Italian dressing***	1 tablespoon
Lard	1 teaspoon
Mayonnaise***	1 teaspoon
Salad dressing, mayonnaise type***	2 teaspoons
Salt pork	3/4 inch cube

   *Made with corn, cottonseed, safflower, soy or sunflower oil only
  **Fat content is primarily monounsaturated
***If made with corn, cottonseed, safflower, soy or sunflower oil
    can be used on fat modified diet

Index